United States
Department of
Agriculture

Forest Service

Pacific Northwest
Research Station

General Technical
Report
PNW-GTR-747
April 2008

Emergent Lessons From a Century of Experience With Pacific Northwest Timber Markets

Richard W. Haynes

Author

Richard W. Haynes (now retired) was a research forester, U.S. Department of Agriculture, Forest Service, Pacific Northwest Research Station, Forestry Sciences Laboratory, P.O. Box 3890, Portland, OR 97208.

Abstract

Haynes, Richard W. 2008. Emergent lessons from a century of experience with Pacific Northwest timber markets. Gen. Tech. Rep. PNW-GTR-747. Portland, OR: U.S. Department of Agriculture, Forest Service, Pacific Northwest Research Station. 45 p.

Timber markets in the United States are areas where timber prices tend to be uniform because of the continuous interactions of buyers and sellers. These markets are highly competitive, volatile, and change relentlessly. This paper looks at how market interactions in the Pacific Northwest have responded to changes in underlying determinants of market behavior and government actions that have influenced supply or demand. Several messages emerge from timber markets about price reporting and changing definitions of price, long-term price trends, timber as an investment, impacts of market intervention, relations among different markets, and implications for future stewardship. The enduring message is that landowners and managers respond to price signals arising from market interactions, and their actions create the forests inherited by future generations.

Keywords: Timber markets, stumpage prices.

Contents

Introduction

Timber markets in the United States usually are thought of as areas where timber prices tend to be uniform because of the continuous interactions of buyers and sellers. These timber markets are powerful institutions and work with nearly invisible structure beyond agreements about terms of trade, including standardization of units. Market interactions reveal how prices and quantities respond to changes in both the underlying determinants of market behavior and government actions that influence supply or demand. Economists often consider prices as a proxy for all market activity in those markets that can be assumed to be competitive. In that role, prices act as a signal to both producers and consumers about prospective levels of supply and demand. If consumers judge current prices to be high, they may reduce purchases. Those same prices seen by producers may lead them to expand production of a good. Such interactions among producers and consumers tend to reward the most efficient producers and to lower costs to consumers.

Here, I summarize some of the messages that emerge from nearly a century of stumpage price data available for the Pacific Northwest (PNW) (see app. 1 for these long-term data sets). This narrative unfolds in several steps. First, I cover some background important to the story. The first part of which is a brief review of the underlying assumptions that help define some of the economic processes and that govern market functions. The second part of the background is a brief overview of the forest industry sector with emphasis on the softwood lumber sector. Second, I summarize some of the key issues that have emerged from timber markets over the past century. These include price reporting and changing definitions of price, long-term price trends, timber as an investment, impacts of market intervention, relations among different markets both spatial and product, and implications for future stewardship. All of these factors provide context for the interpretation of price signals currently described by market interactions. It is these signals that will help guide land use to its highest and best use and stewardship decisions that will shape the forests inherited by future generations.

Much of the ensuing discussion centers on price data from the PNW because as a region it has a relatively long history (within the context of managed forests) of information about its competitive stumpage markets. These markets emerged along with the industrialization of softwood lumber manufacturing following the Civil War and the development of a railroad-based distribution system for sawn wood. Softwood lumber production grew rapidly (see fig. 1) in both the Douglas-fir region (western Oregon and Washington) of the PNW and the United States as a whole. This rapid increase in lumber production stimulated the development of stumpage markets along with price reporting, a multitude of participants, and associations

Timber markets are defined by the interactions of buyers and sellers.

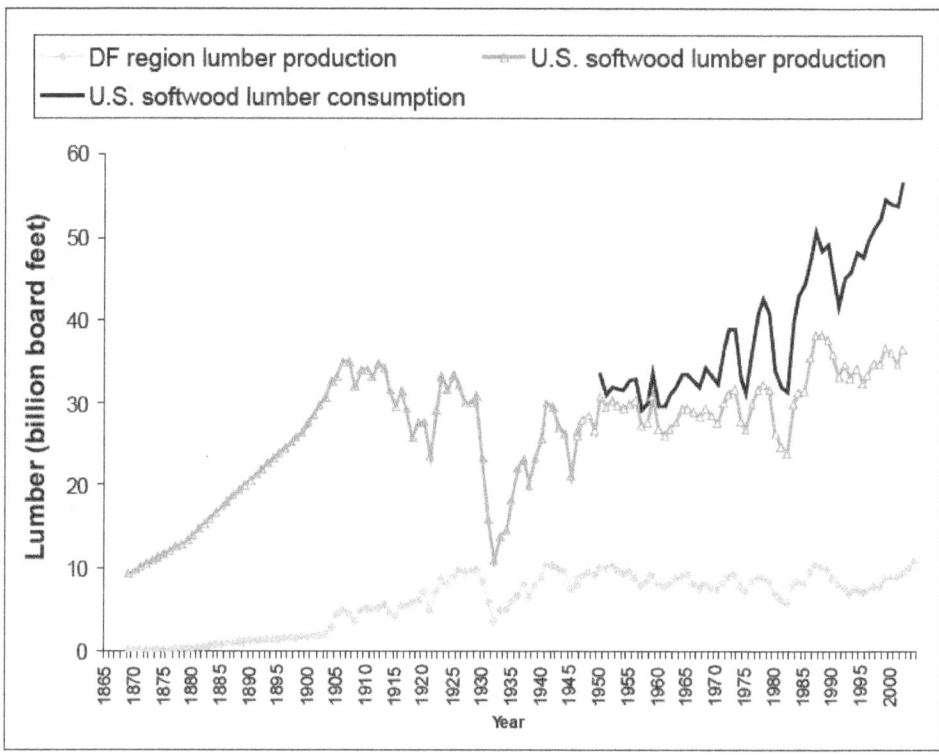

Figure 1—U.S. and Douglas-fir (DF) region lumber production and U.S. lumber consumption.

who established and monitored standard grades. Much of this had all emerged by the early 1900s. The highly volatile stumpage prices shown in figure 2 illustrate the competitive nature of these markets suggesting the absence of other pricing models representing less competition (e.g., where there might be some degree of collusion among buyers and sellers).

Timber markets in the PNW differ from those elsewhere in the United States in two important aspects. First, public land makes up nearly half of the timberland. In spite of the extent of ownership, the proportion of total harvest from public lands has varied as shown in figure 3. But active public timber sales programs have given us a wealth of data that can be used to examine a variety of market issues. The second aspect is the high proportion of harvest from forest industry timberlands. These timberlands provide the resource base for a number of vertically integrated forest product firms that produce a wide variety of forest products.

Background

Two areas of background provide context to the discussion. First, several key economic assumptions underlie many of the points discussed later. These are as-sumptions made generally by economists to simplify the complex pattern of events

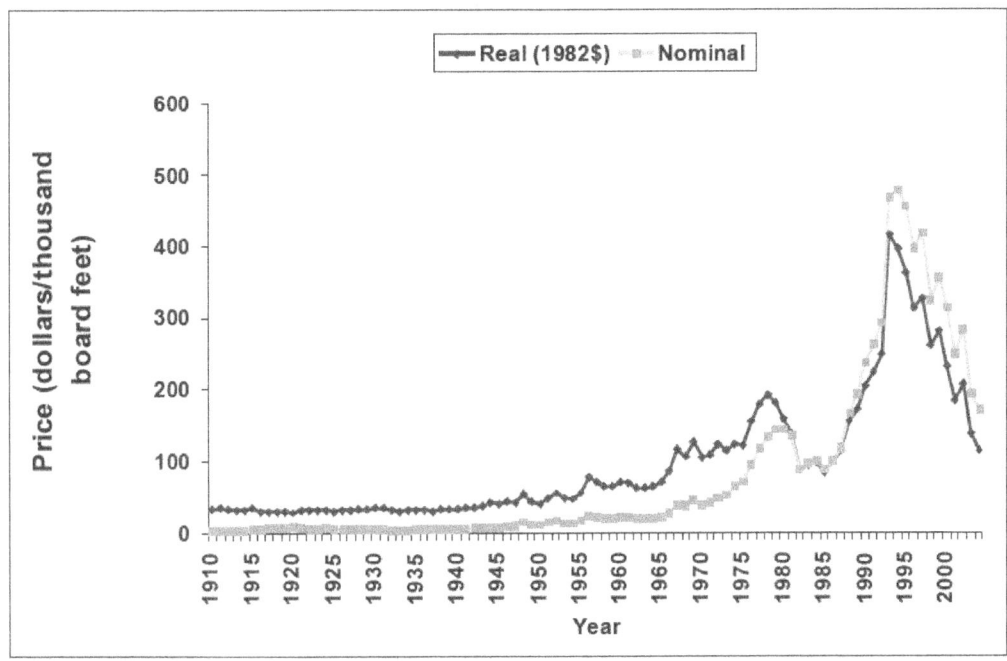

Figure 2—Douglas-fir stumpage price, deflated and nominal.

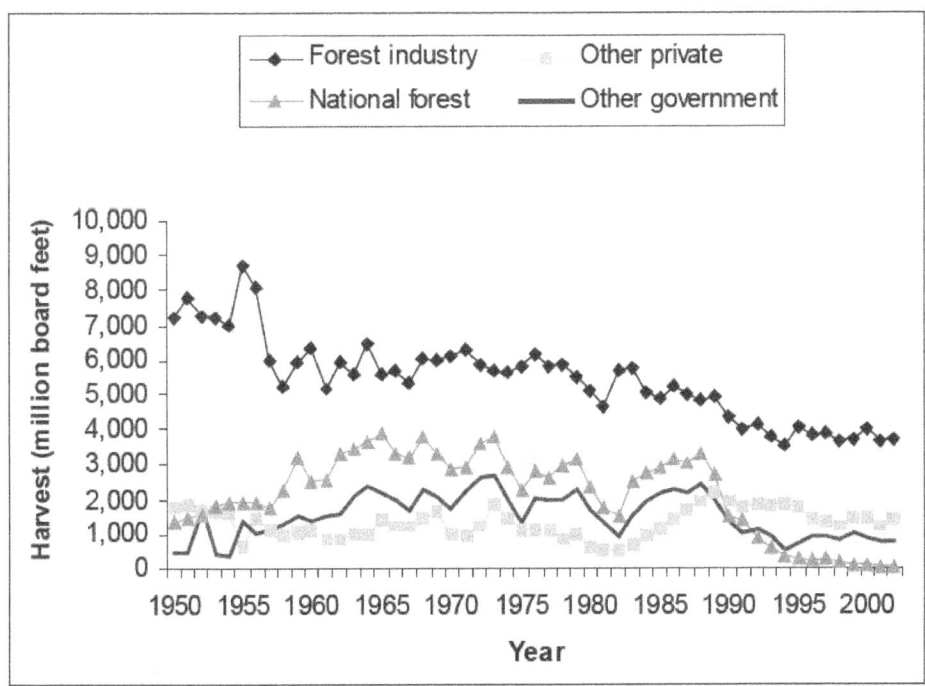

Figure 3—Harvest for the Douglas-fir region, by ownership.

observed in daily life. Second, a brief history of the development and current conditions in the processing industry provides context for how changes in the mix of the products can influence stumpage prices.

Economic Assumptions

Although the idea of a market is among the most basic concepts of economics, its precise definition is problematic (Fackler and Goodwin 2001). Economists consider markets not so much as a physical place but as something that happens virtually as buyers and sellers of a product continually interact. However, the way in which price and quantity data are collected often formalizes both temporal and spatial specificity. For example, we have since the 1960s reported prices for the PNW that represent timber sales data from the 19 national forests composing the PNW Region (Region 6) of the Forest Service, U.S. Department of Agriculture (e.g., see table 94 in Warren 2006).

Key aspects of markets are the economic processes of supply and demand (see app. 2 for a description of price setting and related market constructs). Key also in the case of timber markets is the relation between product and factor markets. That is, timber along with labor and capital are considered factors in the production of, say, lumber or plywood. The simultaneous solution of both markets determines factor prices and quantities along with product prices and quantities.

Economists often assume competitive markets. That is, a market where individual buyers or sellers do not influence the price by their purchases or sales. Four conditions generally describe competitive markets. Buyers and sellers have "perfect" knowledge of prices for other transactions and negligible search costs. There are a large number of buyers and sellers and they act independently. The product is homogenous and divisible. Finally, market entry or exit is easy. Most economic texts discuss the acceptance of these conditions and how the robustness of most markets suggests that extreme assumptions are not necessary to ensure competitive conditions. It is sufficient if traders in a market know of other buyers and sellers and if each trader has knowledge of prevailing prices so that at any one time there is a recognized single price (sometimes called the law of one price).

Markets are thought to be promoters of efficiency. That is, prices and responses to price signals are key elements in how economic efficiency is developed. If prices for something rise, than consumers reduce consumption and vice versa. Producers expecting sustained price increases will seek capital to expand production attempting to capitalize on the higher prices. Consumers expecting sustained price increases will seek alternatives to substitute for the more expensive product.

There is also uncertainty about the extent that spatially separated regions actively compete. This is the essential ingredient of economic models of trade. When there is the opportunity for open exchange (trade) among spatially distinct producers and consumers, there is parity among prices. This parity is the result of market arbitrage where the opportunity for trade among spatially distinct producers and consumers ensures a consistency among spatial patterns of prices (see Fackler and Goodwin 2001 for a review of spatial price analysis).

Market arbitrage is a useful construct for understanding timber markets. Stumpage used in the manufacture of forest products is produced over an extensive spatial area and relatively costly because of its weight to transport. These characteristics like those for other agricultural commodities yield a complex set of spatial price linkages, which give insights into the performance of and relations among stumpage markets. For example, later we will consider the markets for sawtimber and chips in the West. We have detailed data for the softwood sawtimber market and only limited data for chip markets. Nevertheless, by knowing that they share the same larger market we are able to infer price levels for the chip markets in areas where data are limited. This is a powerful tool in developing price proxies where we lack market data.

Economic historians like David Fischer (1996) argued that price revolutions define or are defined by the rhythms of history. In Fischer's view, prices are an indicator that not only illustrates market behavior but offers general insights into otherwise incomparable events. He would look at figure 2 and argue that it illustrates a history of numerous changes in the forest sector. It shows that prices tend both to rise overall and to rise in waves reflecting economic and social changes. But the record of price changes tells many stories in addition to those about changes in underlying determinants of supply and demand.

Whereas the distinction between real and nominal price changes is often not considered by most people, economists assume that individual consumers respond only to real changes in prices and are able to discern those from nominal changes.[1] These real price changes are those in addition to the overall changes in the general price level from inflation. For stumpage prices, this means that landowners and stumpage buyers can estimate the effects of overall price changes as they consider supply and demand forces for timber.

---

[1] That is, economists assume that there is no money illusion where producers or consumers respond to illusionary changes in nominal prices.

The Industry

The forest products industry was among the earliest manufacturing industries to evolve in the PNW. The industry was initially based on processing large (old-growth) trees located near tidewater into lumber for a variety of markets. It rapidly expanded in the 20th century (see fig. 1) with the development of railroads that served domestic and export markets and was an early adopter of advanced materials handling and processing technologies. By 1930, mills in the Douglas-fir region accounted for a third of all U.S. lumber production. Production was based on large relatively clear logs available from private landowners. The main product was Douglas-fir (see "Species List" for scientific names) lumber, and it commanded a price premium relative to other species because it was relatively knot free. Federal logs played a relatively small role because of efforts by the forest industry to restrict federal harvests in order to improve stumpage prices and forest management on private timberlands (see Mason 1969 for details).

However, public harvests rapidly increased following World War II as softwood lumber demand reached new heights and private timber supplies started to decline. From the late 1940s until the late 1980s, timber harvest in the Douglas-fir region increased by roughly 25 percent, fueled mostly by a surge in harvesting on public lands (see fig. 3) (Adams et al. 2006). Between 1945 and 1965, timber harvest on Forest Service land in the western forests of Oregon and Washington rose from about 149 million cubic feet (745 million board feet) to 807 million cubic feet (4,035 million board feet).

During the last 60 years, the industry diversified (see fig. 4) to include the production of a variety of products based both on roundwood harvest from the region's forest as well as products (like paper) based on the residues from primary production. Stumpage used for lumber production fell from 76 percent in 1950 to 38 percent in 1979. The impact of this fall in saw-log demand on stumpage prices was muted by the increase in log exports that helped maintain harvest of saw logs. The log export trade grew rapidly (see fig. 4) as economic growth in Pacific Rim countries provided expanding markets for U.S. timber. During the 1970s and 1980s, log exports on average accounted for roughly 20 percent of timber harvested, and both the domestic and export markets contributed to wide price swings in stumpage markets.

The rise and fall of the log export market would play a particularly important role in the management of the region's private timberlands and for state lands in Washington (from which logs were exportable until the 1990s). Export markets

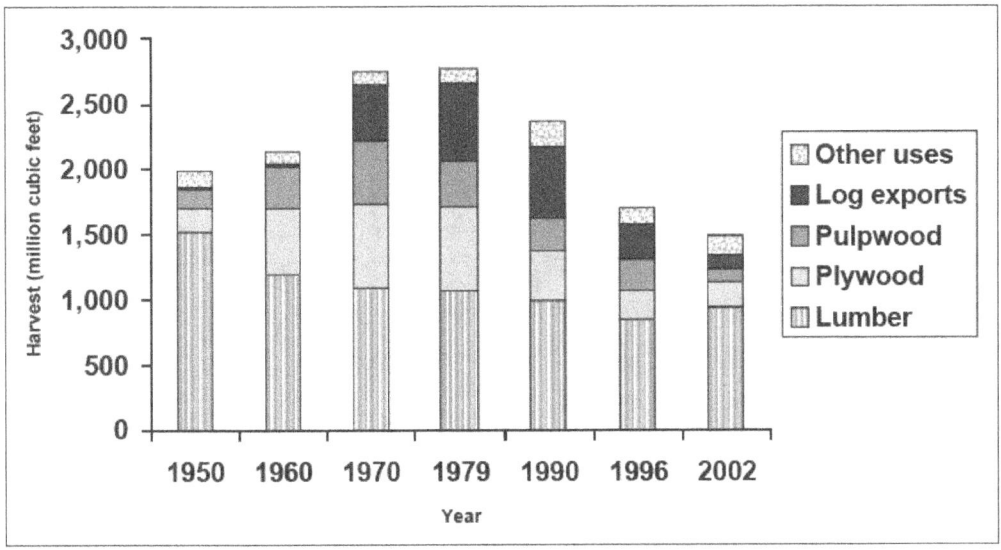

Figure 4—Proportion of Douglas-fir region softwood harvest by product category.

favored larger, older, high-quality trees.[2] By the mid 1980s, old growth on private timberlands was largely exhausted (see Haynes 1986), and log exports came from older second-growth stands that were established following the early industrial harvests. The higher log export prices provided an incentive for some private landowners to manage for longer rotations. This had the ancillary ecological benefit of increasing the proportion of mature forests (older than 60 years) on some private lands, particularly nonindustrial private forest lands. By the early 1980s, effectively all of the old-growth forests on industrial private land and most of the old-growth on nonindustrial private forest land had already been harvested (Haynes 1986). In fact, the proportion of the private inventory composed of trees >160 years old dropped from 15 to less than 1 percent during the 1970s and 1980s (Barbour et al. 2006).

The determinants of the industry's expansion were processing improvements, expansion of Pacific Rim markets for softwood logs, and growth in domestic markets. The rapid growth in harvests and competition among markets led to rapid rises in stumpage prices (see fig. 2) and to bans on exporting federal logs without further processing. By the late 1980s, the industry was bifurcated with a rapidly growing segment of highly efficient mills that cut roughly uniform log mixes of mostly second-growth private timber for commodity markets. Another segment included a number of older and somewhat less efficient mills that processed larger

The diversity of manufacturing in the PNW has declined since 1990.

---

[2] For Douglas-fir, this is usually seen as a mix of stem straightness, cylindrical boles, relatively small infrequent branches (or no branches in older trees), and high stiffness compared to other softwoods.

(and older) log mixes mostly from public timberlands for a range of markets including high-quality domestic and export markets. The design of the older mills made them difficult to adapt to major changes that would soon shape the industry.

The landmark changes started in 1991 with injunctions on the sale of federal timber that were resolved with the implementation of the Northwest Forest Plan (NWFP) (USDA and USDI 1994). The reductions in federal sales caused wood supplies to fall below existing processing capacity and led to mill closures, especially those dependent on federal timber, as many could not efficiently process smaller logs (less than 20 inches) available from private landowners. Demand for log exports also fell as the Japanese economy and then other Asian economies collapsed (Daniels 2005). There have been painful adjustments in the PNW. United States consumers saw little change as the harvest decline (roughly 5 billion board feet) was offset by a combination of factors including harvest increases on private timberlands, increases in harvest in other regions, particularly the U.S. South and the interior Canadian Provinces.[3] Prices did spike upward in 1993 (see Sohngen and Haynes 1994) causing some market dislocation and speeding the adoption of engineered wood products in place of some solid wood products. In addition, the collapse of the log export market from PNW led timber managers and landowners to shift formerly exported logs (annually, more than 2 billion board feet, log scale) to the domestic market helping the timber industry to adapt to reduced federal harvest flows (see Haynes 2003 for a general discussion).

The timber industry in the Douglas-fir region restructured during the 1990s, evolving into a highly efficient but less product-diverse industry, focusing on lumber production from 14- to 20-inch logs primarily for the domestic market and using timber from private timberlands (see Barbour et al. 2003, Haynes and Fight 2004). By one measure, the product diversity increased from 1950 to 1979 by 16 percent but by 2002 fell back to levels nearly the same as in 1950.[4] Much of this change is attributable to the decrease in the proportion of logs being used for lumber production, as both plywood production and log exports increased until the 1990s and then fell as proportion of wood used for lumber rebounded to near the 1960 levels (see fig. 4).

---

[3] These shifts validated the warnings of those who said that federal protection for the northern spotted owl (*Strix occidentalis caurina*) would shift the environmental consequences elsewhere. Economists call these types of effects "unintended consequences" and often argue that they demonstrate policy failures in the sense of not having considered the full range of possible effects.

[4] This was computed by using the Shannon Weaver diversity index and the data from figure 4. The region's product diversity peaked in 1990.

The loss of product diversity described earlier has implications for stumpage prices. Earlier studies of bidding (see Haynes 1980) found that higher bid prices for stumpage were often associated with a larger number of bidders who represented a wider range of forest products and markets. The proposition was that the greater the diversity of products produced the higher was the likelihood of some bidder being willing to bid more given their unique products. The opposite argument, and perhaps what we are seeing now, is that if most producers produce nearly the same thing, (such as commodity grades of softwood lumber) then there are fewer opportunities for unique market niches and consequently lower overall stumpage prices.

The sawmills, themselves, have changed rapidly. Currently there is little capacity capable of handling logs over 24 inches in diameter, but there is an evolving small-log industry using logs between 4.5 and 10 inches small-end diameter. Mills themselves are changing with the development of both very large mills (producing 300,000 to 400,000 board feet per shift) and specialty mills, some of which are relatively small (less than 50,000 board feet per shift). It is still a large industry. In 2002, 13.44 billion board feet of lumber was produced in Washington, Oregon, and California requiring 1.68 billion cubic feet of logs or 1.4 million truckloads. The surviving and new mills are in locations along main transportation corridors and close to private timberlands. Now some rural areas formerly thought of as timber dependent have little local forest products manufacturing, and logs harvested in the area are shipped to manufacturing centers further away resulting in slightly lower stumpage prices than in the past and reduced employment in spite of relatively high harvests.

The softwood lumber industry is characterized as being highly competitive. Evidence of this included the widespread use of a simple national price for softwood lumber in various statistical reports. Support for this assertion is also the relatively low degree of concentration of production among the largest producers. In 2006, the four largest companies in North America accounted for 25 percent of all softwood lumber production manufactured at 91 mills. The next four largest firms added another 11 percent of lumber production manufactured at 60 mills.[5] Other evidence includes what is essentially a single national price for commodity grades of lumber.

Changes in product markets during the 1990s contributed to highly volatile stumpage markets as landowners and forest products producers adjusted to the reductions in federal timber flows (see Warren 2004, for various data series, and Haynes et al. 2007 for a discussion of regional and national market adjustments).

---

[5] This was computed from lumber production data reported in Random Lengths Yardstick (2007).

Since the mid 1990s, stumpage prices have been stable or declining (recall fig. 2), suggesting lower financial returns to various forestry practices. These lower prices together with the loss of the export price premium have reduced the price expectations of landowners and may threaten commitments to sustainable forest management by some landowners. These relatively weak stumpage prices are leading to a shift toward forest management regimes that favor shorter rotations (Haynes 2005). Today the economic incentive for all private landowners is to grow smaller, more uniform trees. One consequence of this is a divergence between ecological conditions on public and private timberland (see fig. 70 in Haynes 2003 and a discussion of ecological consequences in Spies 2006).

Market Messages

Timber markets have operated for the past century with little regulatory oversight.

Stumpage markets in the Douglas-fir region have operated over the past century as unregulated entities and, other than for some common scaling rules, operate without oversight. These are competitive markets and as such can be used to illustrate a wide range of economic issues including price reporting, spatial price variation, long-term price trends, the effects of different types of market intervention, persistence of price premiums reflecting higher quality, and the relation of stumpage and product markets. The robustness of this market can be used to illustrate other economic circumstances. For example, from the 1960s to the 1990s, the log export restrictions on federal logs resulted in dual markets for domestic and export logs.[6] Since the collapse of the export markets in the late 1990s, export prices have adjusted to those in domestic markets. Another example is the extensive insights about how bidders respond to different sale characteristics and changes in sales practices (e.g., Haynes 1980, Mead 1966). These insights were developed using the extensive data sets of federal timber sales that included appraisal data, bidding data, and some information about those bidding for federal timber.

Reported Stumpage Prices

In most markets, the multiplicity of buyers, sellers, and transactions obscure prices and threaten the one-price condition necessary to ensure competitive markets. Various institutions with a vested interested in ensuring competitive markets often step in by providing price reporting to help inform both buyers and sellers. In the United States, there are two conventions for reporting stumpage prices. First, there is reporting of actual transaction prices based on actual stumpage sales that often

---

[6] Some observe that the export market may not have been as competitive as the domestic market as it was dominated at times by a few large exporters or trading firms.

use some sort of bidding process. The reported prices are volume-weighted averages of the species or species groups offered for sale. That is, they are the average of the species making up the sales offered in a particular location during a given period. The weights are the volume proportions for each species. Consider the example in table 1. These are prices for sawtimber sold on the national forests in the Northern Region (Region 1) during 2004. The values and volumes are annual data reflecting prices and sales volumes reported by quarter (see table 80 in Warren 2006 for the actual data) where the quarterly variation in 2004 was from $146 to $221. The right-most column shows the volume weights and suggests that the prices for Douglas-fir and true fir will largely determine the regional price.

The use of transaction data from Forest Service sales has led to two measures of stumpage prices. The most widely reported stumpage prices are the prices bid for USDA Forest Service timber sales. These prices have been published quarterly since 1963 for broad areas and are generally cited as "sold" or "bid" prices. They

Table 1—Construction of volume-weighted stumpage price, Northern Region, 2004

Species	Value	Volume	Volume weight
	Dollars/thousand board feet	*Thousand board feet*	*Percent*
Cedar	169.78	2,773	1.8
Douglas-fir	172.09	58,845	38.4
Engelmann spruce	204.05	5,264	3.4
Larch	146.44	13,548	8.8
Lodgepole pine	163.91	28,845	18.8
Ponderosa pine	126.71	1,987	1.3
True fir	121.25	39,044	25.5
Western hemlock	113.45	309	.2
Western white pine	129.60	2,723	1.8
All species	154.93	153,338	

represent the high bid for timber sales. The other measure is the price paid for timber harvested from Forest Service sales. This price is called the "cut" or "harvest" price and for an individual sale is the adjusted high-bid price[7] when logs are scaled after harvest. The cut price series is available only as an all-species average, whereas sold prices are available for both principal species and all-species averages. In both cases, the averages are most commonly reported as volume weighted as illustrated in table 1.

The drawback to the use of Forest Service sales data is that it is for a fairly generic mix of log grades that have changed in definition over the past century. Although individual bidders do adjust their bids to reflect their perceptions of sale quality (based on species and differences in log grades, see Haynes 1980 for details), there is no way to adjust sale prices over time for changes in the quality of logs being sold. One concern is the extent Forest Service prices represent market prices. For the Douglas-fir region, Adams and Haynes (1989) found that harvest (cut) prices were representative of market prices in the post-World War II period. During that period, however, the Forest Service sold mostly old-growth and mature timber while private landowners increasingly sold younger and smaller sawtimber (see table 14 in Haynes 2005 to assess this trend). Since the reduction of federal harvest because of the Northwest Forest Plan, the Forest Service has sold mostly younger timber from either thinning or hazardous fuel reduction activities and the associated lower sale prices reflect this lower quality relative to stumpage available from private timberlands. This concern will be examined in more detail in a later section.

The second type of stumpage prices are list prices. This type of price is collected from various log buyers at specific points in time by a reporting service that then reports averages being paid in a selected region for specific log mixes. In the PNW, Log Lines (2000-2004) is an example of this type of price reporting. In that case, the reported prices are actually prices of logs delivered to mills so that they include both stumpage and logging costs. Another example of delivered log values used in the PNW are log export prices, which are derived from the customs forms filed with the customs districts where the exporting takes place.

Stumpage prices are usually reported in nominal terms and by convention are not seasonally adjusted. Until the early 1980s, nominal prices were the most frequently used to assess market conditions including price forecasting. The

---

[7] Most Forest Service timber sale contacts being offered in the West include provisions for adjusting the stumpage rates actually paid by purchasers because of changes in product selling values. This process is termed "stumpage rate adjustment" or "price escalation." The adoption of "stumpage rate adjustment" provisions varied over time, leading to some distortions in the relation of sold and cut prices when comparing stumpage prices among regions.

disparity, however, in implications for long-term price trends between nominal and real prices demonstrated the need to consider both series. For example, for the period 1950-1975, the nominal price trends suggested that stumpage prices were increasing at 6.4 percent per year. At that rate, we expect stumpage prices to double every 11.25 years. However, adjusting for inflation (and looking only at the real rates of increase) the real rate of increase was 4.3 percent per year during this 25-year period. At this rate, prices double every 16.75 years. The difference between the two trends suggests the need for caution to avoid spurious recommendations based solely on perceived changes in the nominal prices.

Seasonal patterns do exist in stumpage markets, especially in monthly data where there is greater volatility in prices owing to cyclic trends in the market (Haynes 1991). Figure 5 illustrates a comparison of monthly prices both adjusted and unadjusted. Most of volatility in the series seems to be due to cyclic trends in the market. In this case the unadjusted data are still a robust representation of the value of timber, but some caution is needed to acknowledge the extent of seasonal variation.

The monthly data do not display any greater seasonality than do the quarterly stumpage prices traditionally used to describe stumpage markets. For quarterly data, seasonal adjustments for the period 1975-1989 averaged 1.06, 0.98, 0.92, and 1.04 for the first, second, third, and fourth quarters, respectively. That is, on average, prices, in the first quarter (winter) averaged 6 percent higher than the annual average and 15 percent higher than prices in the third quarter (summer). The higher

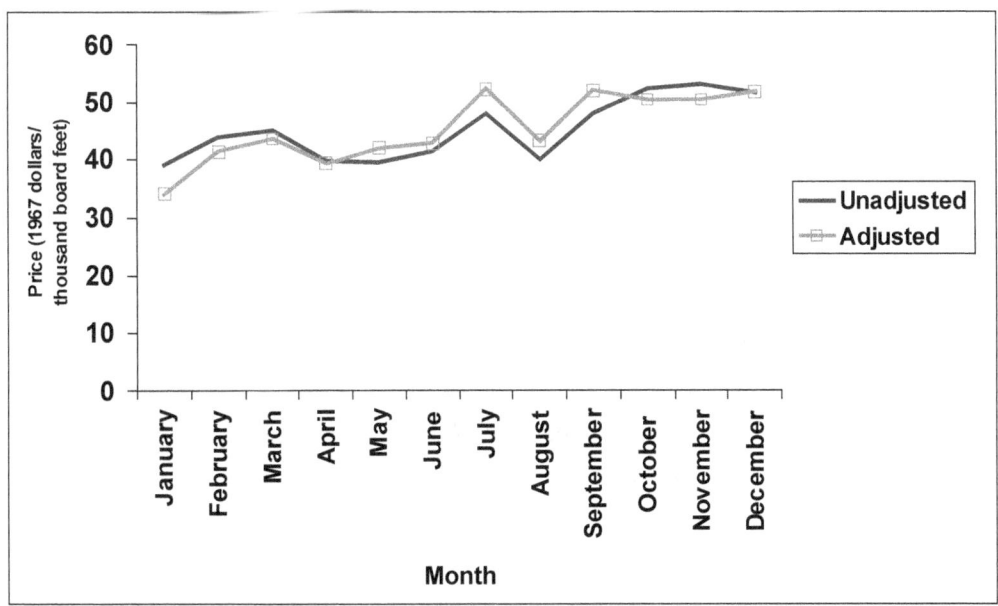

Figure 5—Stumpage price seasonal adjustments (1987).

prices in late fall and winter (fourth and first quarters) reflect the closure of higher elevation logging sites and reduced timber sale offerings. Although the estimates of seasonality suggest the need for some cautions about intra-annual comparisons, custom condones the use of unadjusted price series.

Figures 6a and 6b illustrate several general issues that provide context for the discussion in this section. Figure 6a, for example, shows saw-log prices for three softwood species sold in widely dispersed markets. There is a relatively high degree of correlation among the species. There are also persistent regional differences that reflect differences in logging and manufacturing costs, and in the case of Douglas-fir, some of the higher prices until the late 1980s were because of price premiums enjoyed by Douglas-fir lumber (see Haynes et al. 1988). That these widely dispersed markets vary in tandem responding to the same economic stimulus demonstrates their competitiveness. The relative positions of the prices illustrate the substitutability of the species for each other in many end uses.

To be useful, factor prices like stumpage should track changes in end product markets. That is, sawtimber stumpage prices should mirror what is happening in, say, lumber markets. In case of competitive markets, these prices should also reflect major exogenous changes in the stumpage markets. For example, the reduction in federal harvest in the PNW following the implementation of the NWFP (USDA and USDI 1994) reduced the total stumpage supply function inducing changes as competitive pressures forced adjustments in lumber production. These competitive pressures evolve over several years. They start as rising stumpage prices increase manufacturing costs and reduce profitability. Reduced profitability leads to production cutbacks as manufacturers attempt to balance production with sales. This adjustment process continues until lower production levels lead to a balance between the supply and demand and more stable prices. This process is illustrated in figure 6a where there are rapid stumpage price increases (following the harvest reductions on federal lands in the early 1990s) followed by a decrease in prices as production adjusts downward and prices between regions are more aligned (for the example, the prices for Douglas-fir and southern pine 2000-2004).

Spatial Variation

There is considerable spatial variation in stumpage prices. As an example, consider average stumpage prices for each of the nine contiguous national forests that line the Cascade Mountains in Washington and Oregon. These average prices are shown in figure 7 for the forests aligned from north to south. There are several reasons often cited to explain these differences including differences in species, stand volumes, local processing opportunities, amount of private timber available for

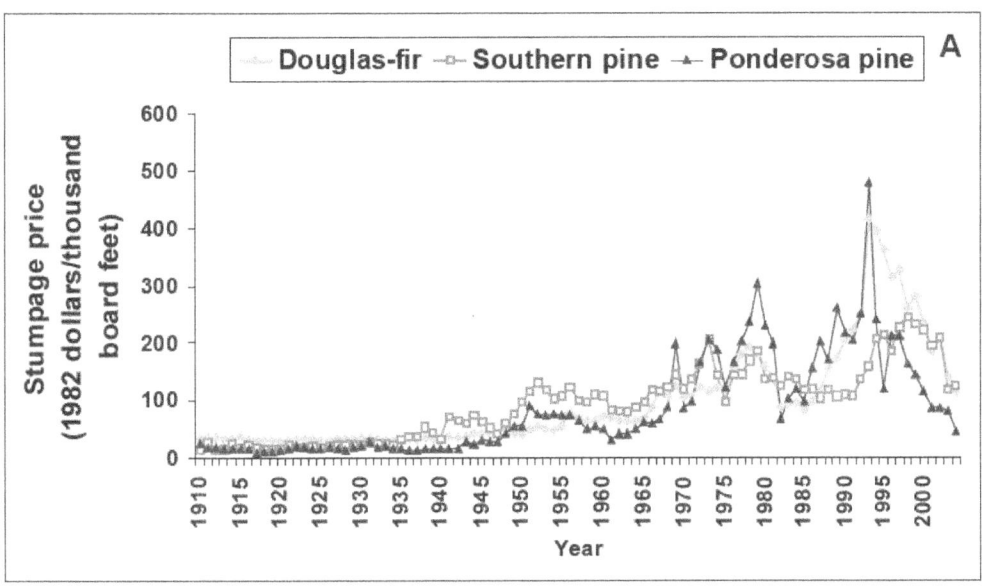

Figure 6a—Stumpage prices for Douglas-fir, ponderosa pine, and southern pine.

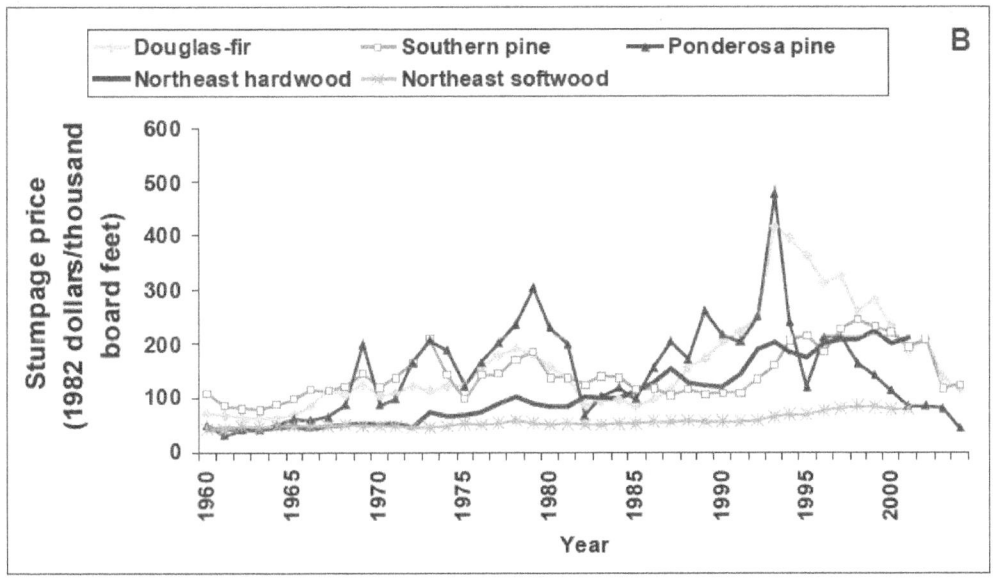

Figure 6b—Stumpage prices for Douglas-fir, ponderosa pine, southern pine, Northeast softwood, and Northeast hardwood.

harvest, access (specifically the costs to build or rebuild roads), and localized differences in sale preparation and administration. Even controlling for these factors, we would expect to see differences in stumpage prices that reflect the spatial dispersion of timber supplies from available processing centers. These local differences would be explained by differences in transportation costs from the location of production (in the case of forests—the stand) to the point of processing. This is the classic case of site prices described by Bressler and King (1970) and shown in figure 8. Here the

15

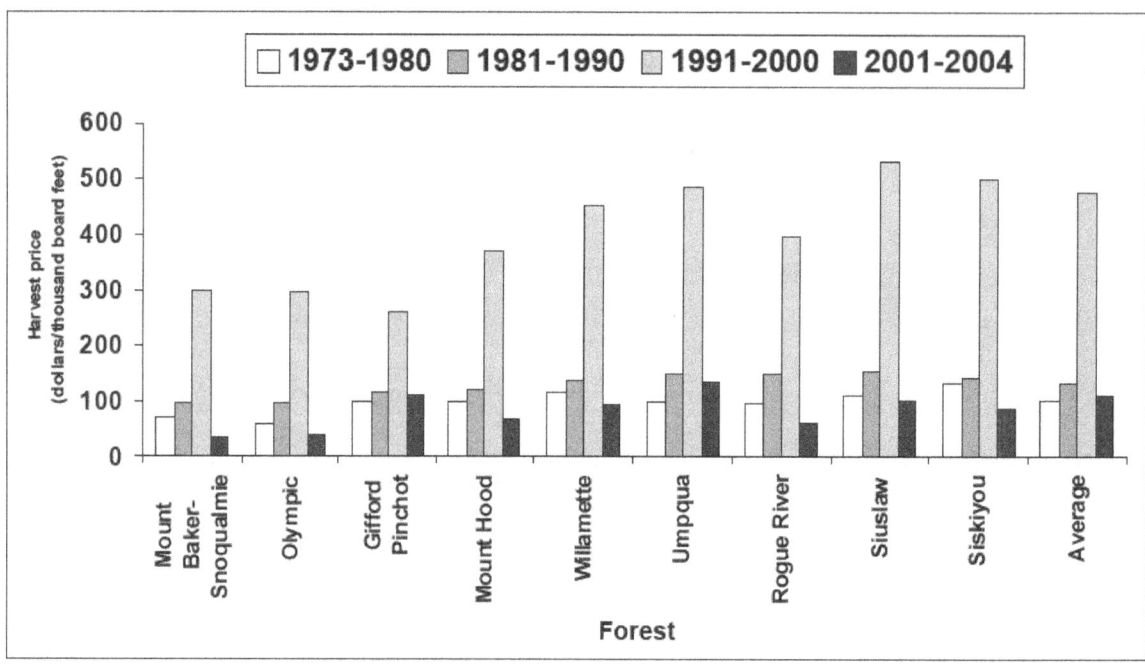

Figure 7—Stumpage price for timber harvested from the national forests of the Pacific Northwest-west.

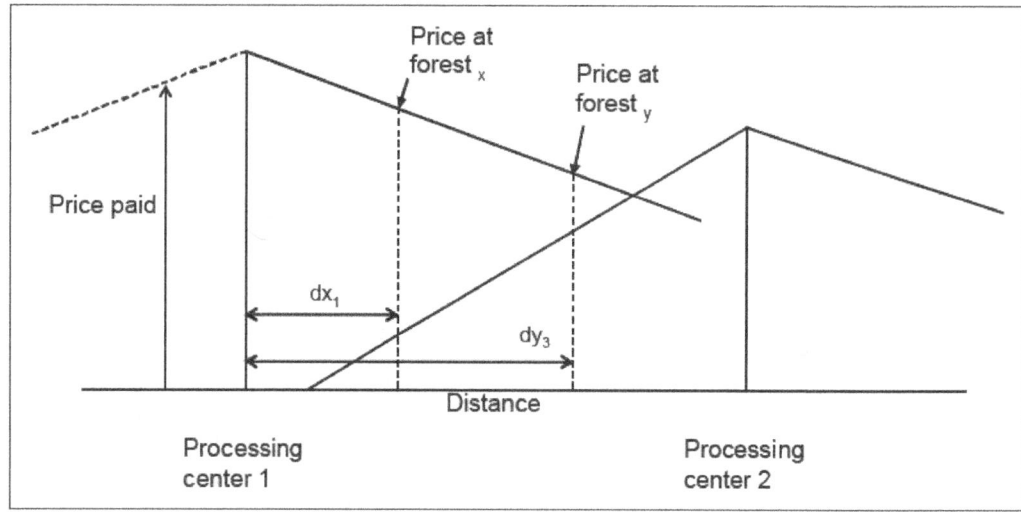

Figure 8—Relation of stumpage prices and distance to processing centers.

difference in prices between forest x and y (P_x - P_y) would be equal to the additional transport cost ([dy_3 - dx_1] x cost [usually expressed on a per-mile basis]). If prices in the second processing center were to increase to equal those in the first processing center, timber prices on forest y would be greater by the difference between the price line for processing center 1 and the upward revised price line from processing center 2.

Market arbitrage limits the difference between stumpage prices. For example the stumpage prices of the nine nearly contiguous national forests aligned along the Coast and Cascades Range in Washington and Oregon ranged in 1993 from $164 to $411 per thousand board feet. The average price was $348 per thousand board feet. Figure 7 illustrates that being close to the major softwood lumber manufacturing facilities in the Willamette Valley, especially its southern end, increases prices for the local national forests (Willamette, Umpqua, and Sisuslaw). That pattern is relatively consistent over the past four decades, but there are differences in earlier periods when the forests adjacent to the Columbia River offered attractive markets (like the situation shown in fig. 8).

Stumpage prices have experienced real price increases for the last century.

Long-Term Price Trends

The underlying data shown in figures 6 and 9 are being used by various investors[8] and land management organizations to demonstrate the attractiveness of timberland investments. As investments, timberlands complement stock and other financial in-

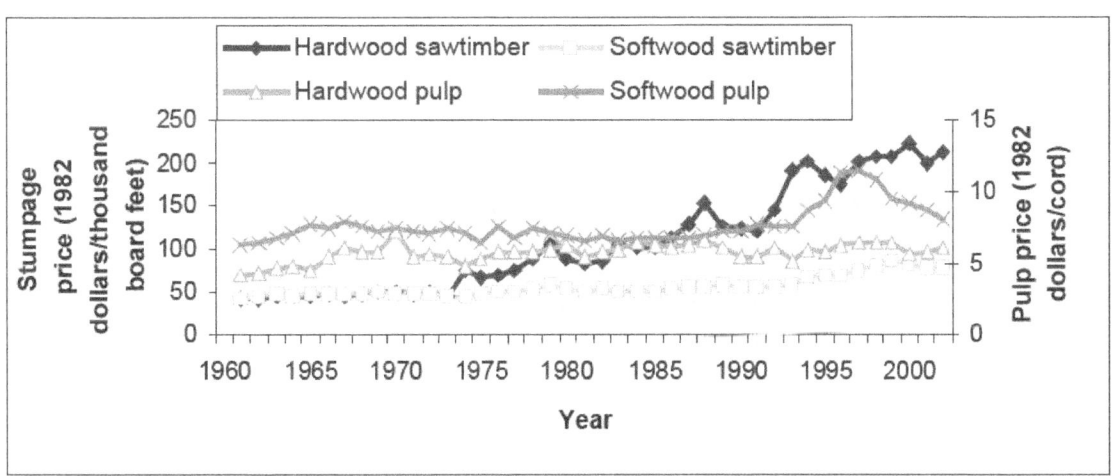

Figure 9—Northeastern sawtimber stumpage and pulp prices.

struments, but the tendency of stock portfolios to drop as well as changes in the tax laws have made timberland attractive to large institutional investors (see Hancock Timber Resource Group 2003, Thompson 1997). The rates of return for timberland investments are often higher than for alternative investments, but the volatility in prices gives timber a higher variability. Thompson (1997) found that holding a fixed 10-percent of a portfolio in timber showed about a 1-percent higher rate of return with no increase in risk compared to portfolios with no timber.

[8] Including timber investment management organizations (TIMOs).

Figures 6a and 6b show a history of change. These series illustrate that stumpage prices tend to rise overall and that much of the increase typically comes in waves consistent with structural shifts in underlying markets. These series illustrate long-term real increases of 2.7 percent per year for Douglas-fir and 3.0 percent per year for southern pine. For the past 50 years, these rates are 3.5 percent per year and 1.3 percent per year, respectively.[9] The average deviation from the trends for each decade until the 1950s was 2 to 11 percent for Douglas-fir and 5 to 14 percent for southern pine. In the last six decades this deviation has been larger as shown in the following tabulation.

Average deviation by decade from trend prices

Year	Douglas-fir	Southern pine
	Percent	
1950	12	45
1960	17	17
1970	25	37
1980	37	37
1990	106	36

Until the 1990s, there was always greater variation in the South than in the West, but the greater volatility since 1950 reflects a period when timber demands rose faster than supplies and regional production shifted first to the West and then back to the South (see the Resource Planning Act timber assessments for a discussion of these changes [Haynes and Adams 2007]).

Table 2 presents rates of price appreciation for the series shown in figures 6 and 9. All of these figures are real rates of price appreciation and demonstrate that, in addition to the price volatility discussed earlier, there are significant long-term real price increases. At the same time, however, the changes in timber markets in the 1990s have fundamentally altered these long-term price trends, and recent stumpage price projections (Haynes et al. 2007) suggest only modest growth for the next five decades. These more modest price increases raise concerns about the prospects for sustainable forest management where the adoption of management practices by some owners depend on continuously rising prices (see Haynes 2007 for a more detailed discussion).

---

[9] These are computed from the coefficient A_2 estimated from the following regression:
ln (price) = A_1 + A_2 x time.

Table 2—Rates of real price appreciation for stumpage

Years	Sawtimber		
	Douglas-fir	**Ponderosa pine**	**Southern pine**
	Percent		
1910-2004	2.6	3.3	2.9
1910-1990	2.4	4.0	3.3
1991-2004	-6.7	-13.3	0

	Northeast			
	Hardwood sawtimber	**Hardwood pulpwood**	**Softwood sawtimber**	**Softwood pulpwood**
	Percent			
1961-2002	4.6	0.5	1.3	0.7
1961-1990	4.5	.9	.8	0
1991-2002	3.8	0	3.9	0

From an economic perspective, the general history of rising prices (as shown in figs. 6 and 9) suggests that timber is relatively scarce and, all else being equal, that there should be changes in various market factors to alleviate the price increases. This behavior is expected as these are relatively efficient (free) markets comprising numerous producers and consumers making decisions based on available information. The history of rising prices should also encourage consumers to substitute nonwood material in some uses, such as residential construction (e.g., steel studs for framing), if the real prices of the substitute are less (or more stable) than wood prices. These rising stumpage prices have encouraged increased efficiency and diversity in the mix of forest products as both producers and timberland owners looked for ways to increase returns. Rising prices should also encourage land-owners and managers to increase the intensity or extent of land management to produce more timber (to the point where expected timber prices become stable).

Where Market Intervention Has Made a Difference

There are two examples where different types of market intervention have made a difference in stumpage prices. The first of these is the example of log exports. The volumes of logs exported from the four west coast customs districts are shown in figure 10. The sudden apparent increase in log exports (see Daniels 2005, Darr et al. 1980 for a brief history) in the mid 1960s led to restrictions being placed on log exports from federal lands starting in 1968.

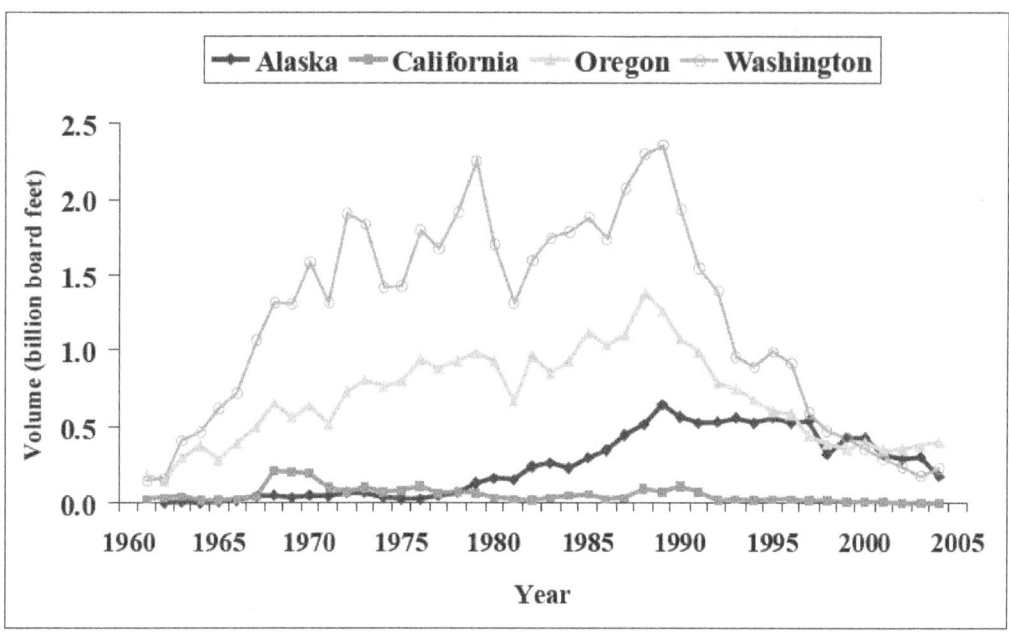

Figure 10—Volume of log exports from the west coast and Alaska.

The expected market responses can be described using conventional economic representations as described in appendix 2. In an economic context, log export restrictions on federal timber reduce overall supply available to the export market and raise stumpage prices for all participants. But in this case it also produces higher prices for owners whose stumpage is exportable and lower prices for owners whose stumpage is limited to the domestic market. This market intervention results in a bifurcated market, and although prices for federal timber are higher than they would be without the opportunity for trade, they are less than they would be in a free market. This intervention also results in higher prices for logs that can be exported leading to windfall gains to some landowners. The difference between prices in the two markets became known as the export premium and was contentious in debates both about export policies and eventually about changes in federal timber flows in the early 1990s.

Part of the controversy was the extent that export price premiums could be verified from existing data. Confounding this problem was that log exports were subject to some postharvest handling (extra sorting for the various export markets) and were reported from customs data as values along ship side (f.a.s.) reflecting stumpage, logging, and these additional handling costs. One way to approximate these premiums in the stumpage market is to compare prices for stumpage from national forests and state forests in western Washington. The Washington Department of Natural Resources (DNR) was active in the log export markets until the early 1990s but sold stumpage roughly similar in quality and using administrative procedures similar to those of national forests.[10] The prices shown in figure 11 illustrate a persistent price difference (1968-1992) that averaged $72 per thousand board feet.

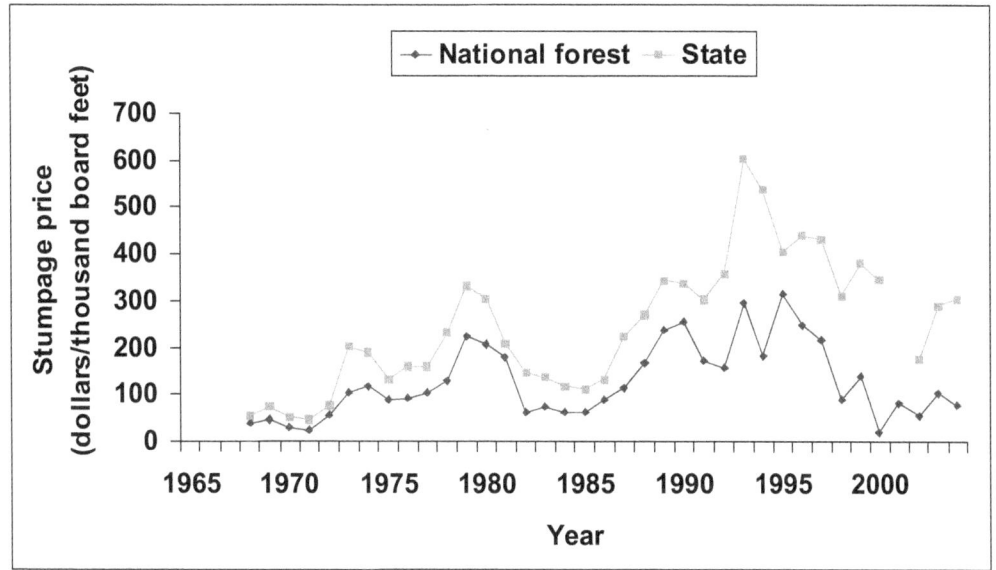

Figure 11—Average stumpage price for national forest and state lands in western Washington.

A second example of market intervention that led to price differences was the small business administration (SBA) set-aside program applied to Forest Service sales. The SBA set-aside program was implemented in the early 1960s in an attempt to ensure that a set percentage (based on historical volumes) of timber sold by the Forest Service went to small businesses (defined as being less than 500 employees). Figure 12 shows the proportion of volume that actually was restricted for sale only to eligible small businesses. For a decade (the early 1970s to 1980s) about 25 percent of the timber sales were restricted to small businesses. In earlier work (1979, 1980), I found that the sales prices for set-aside sales were less than what might be expected for timber sales of that size and quality. At that time, I said that "lower prices for sales of at least equal profitability are symptomatic of restricted competition ... (and) an implicit subsidy to those firms winning set-aside sales" (Haynes 1979: 283).

There is a shorter record of published price data to illustrate this (from 1986 to current), but the data for 1986-1990 suggest that set-aside sales average 2 percent

---

[10] The price differences between national forest and state forests in western Washington after 1992 represent differences in timber qualities. These differences are discussed in a later section.

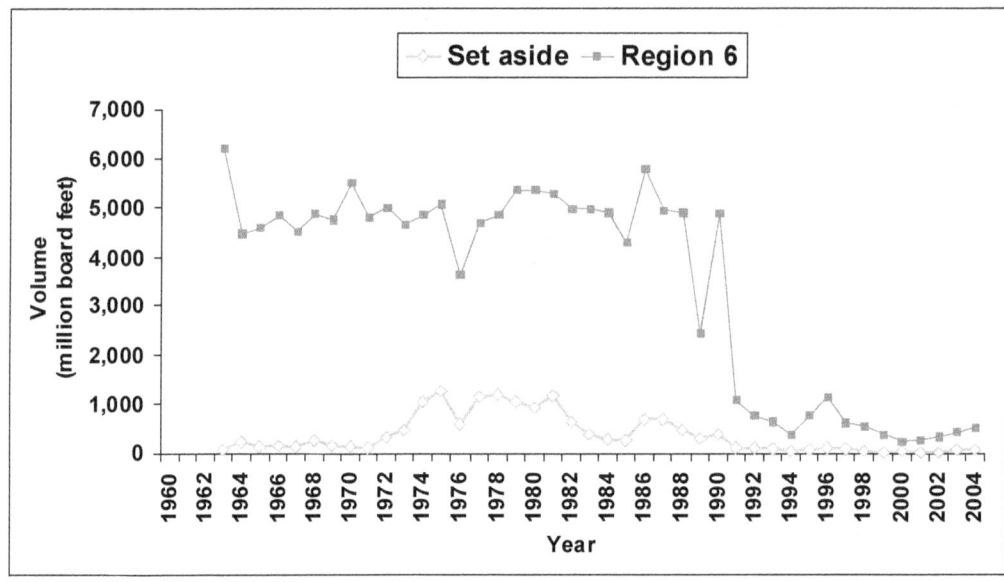

Figure 12—Pacific Northwest national forest timber volume sold for set-aside sales and total Pacific Northwest Region (Region 6).

less than all sales in Region 6. Data for 1975-1978 show a difference between set-aside and open sales for the west-side forests of 6 percent (Haynes 1980).

Both of these cases illustrate the workings of a competitive market in the sense that interventions from either the demand or supply side of the market had predictable outcomes. Both also represent relatively common types of market interventions undertaken for specific reasons but without much consideration of their widespread effects. For example, log export restrictions were initially debated in terms of their employment effects and not their price impacts. When price impacts entered into the debate, they were mostly considered in terms of reductions in returns to landowners and only recently in terms of the positive impacts they might have had on land stewardship. That is, higher prices for larger logs provide incentives for management practices that produce these logs.

The Relation Between Stumpage and Product Markets

Price markup rules—

There has been a long-standing interest in trying to assess conditions in the stumpage market by observing changes in the lumber market. In essence this leads to the relation:

$$P^a = A + BP^x$$

Where

P^a is the stumpage price (log scale),
A and B are estimated coefficients, and
P^x is the price for softwood lumber (lumber scale).

Both P^a and P^x are for the same general species groups. This relation is the conceptual basis behind the residual value appraisal system used by the Forest Service during the late 20th century. The Forest Service is required by law to appraise timber at the "fair market value," and this was seen as providing such an estimate. It was also the basis for considering the stumpage market price effects associated with forest policy discussions, which was common until the mid 1970s. Spelter (2005) recently examined the use of price markup rules to establish estimates of stumpage values that investors could use as a benchmark and as useful leading indicators of reported market directions.

Within the economics literature (see George and King 1971) these are called price markup rules and were originally used to explore the product/factor market relations and how changes in, say, product prices would be transmitted to factor prices. In general, these relations were described as being one of three forms depending on the nature of prices in one market level relative to the other: a fixed markup, a proportional markup, or a combination of the two. These relations can be used to describe the ability to pass through changes in input costs to product prices, or its inverse, the ability to impose changes in product prices on input. This ability is called the elasticity of price transmission and ranges in forest markets depending on species and regions from 0.30 to 0.64 (Haynes 1977, Spelter 2005).

Using the data (for 1910-2002) shown in figure 2, we can estimate the price markup relation for Douglas-fir. Both the intercept and slope coefficients are significant suggesting that this combines both the fixed and variable markup relations (it is a proportional markup). The relation is:

$$P^{df} = -54.85 + 0.71 \; P^{lp}$$

Where P^{df} = stumpage price for Douglas-fir and P^{lp} = price for Douglas-fir lumber.

My original work on price markup rules was intended to disentangle the way in which stumpage prices had been estimated in the 1973 Outlook study (USDA FS 1973). There the authors of the Outlook study had assumed that an average of about 75 percent of future increases in forest product prices would go to stumpage. The remaining 25 percent of product price increases would be available to cover higher costs of harvesting and manufacture (USDA FS 1973: 149). With estimates of the elasticity of price transmission of, say, 0.45, the actual increase in stumpage price would be about 45 percent, considerably less than what was being estimated by the Forest Service.

This relation and the elasticity of price transmission that can be computed from its coefficients also can be used to describe the relation between product and factor (input) demand functions. If we assume that the product production functions are fixed factors, then we can compute the elasticity in the factor demand market as the product of the elasticity in the product market and the elasticity of price transmission (see Haynes 1977). This approach provides a useful way to relate short-term changes in stumpage markets to changes in product markets.

Speed of market adjustments—
Another past concern has been the speed that prices adjust to changes in market conditions. For example, how fast do we see increases in stumpage prices when single-family housing starts (reported monthly) suddenly increase? In this case, the market impact traces from observed increases in reported housing starts (a leading indicator of economic activity) to increases in lumber demand and lumber prices to increases in stumpage prices all reflecting increases in demand for housing. Past research suggests that stumpage prices adjust within 1 to 2 months of changes in product markets and that product markets adjust within a month of changes in underlying market determinants.

There are implications for price reporting in this discussion of how fast prices express market changes. As the adjustment takes place within 1 to 2 months, it is common to use quarterly data as the finest practical resolution for price reporting (e.g., see Warren 2006, Timber Mart-South 2000-2004, Log Lines 2000-2004). This assumes that quarterly prices represent average market conditions in both markets that have adjusted to market signals within the same quarter.

There are also some implications for those who wonder why product and stumpage markets don't display the same variation. First, figures like figure 3 display annual data that obscures the speed of various market adjustments. Second, given the discussion about the elasticity of price transmission, the differences in elasticities between the product and stumpage markets suggest that price changes in the stumpage markets will be greater than those in the product market.

Persistence of Price Premiums for Timber Quality

In addition to the log export price premiums and the persistent differences among species prices, another type of price premiums are those paid for stumpage that will produce a higher proportion of higher grade lumber. Figures 13a and 13b for

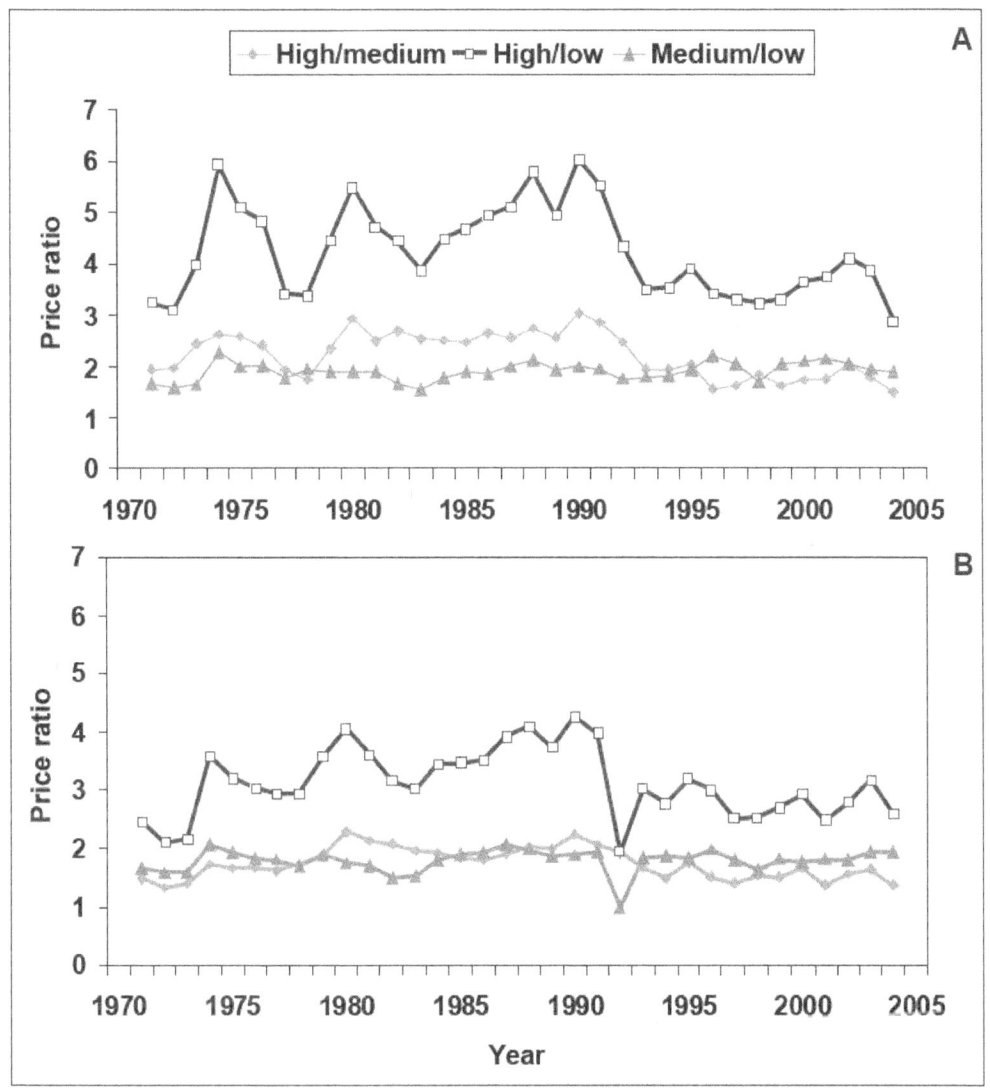

Figure 13—Douglas-fir (a) and coast hem-fir (b) lumber price ratios for grade groups.

Douglas-fir and coast hem-fir of high-to-low or high-to-medium grades of lumber show how price premiums have persisted over the past 35 years. Persistent higher prices for higher grades have been used by advocates of alternative management regimes to argue for high-quality forestry (Barbour et al. 2003, Waggener and Fight 1999, Weigand et al. 1994). The heart of their argument is that management actions that lead to higher quality saw logs that produce a higher proportion of high-grade lumber increase returns to land management. The various management actions involved in high-quality forestry include thinning and pruning strategies and longer rotations coupled with more frequent thinning.

In an earlier paper (Haynes 2005), I estimated that for Douglas-fir, increasing rotation length from 40 to 160 years would increase stumpage value by roughly 5 percent because of increased recovery of higher grades of lumber. This is smaller than the large differences cited by proponents of longer rotation who often look at only differences in lumber prices without considering the relation among stumpage and lumber prices (see the section on the price markup rules for more details).

Another illustration of how timber quality affects stumpage prices is to compare prices in western Washington for timber sold by the Forest Service and by Washington DNR. Both agencies offered roughly similar sales in terms of species, volumes, quality, and operational requirements including offering sales for bid by prospective buyers. Until the early 1990s, Washington DNR timber was exportable and both agencies sold sales that had a mix of older second growth and old growth. Because of the export sales, prices for Washington DNR sales averaged 62 percent more than prices for Forest Service sales. Since 1992, when Washington DNR sales were no longer exportable, Washington DNR prices averaged 152 percent more than prices for Forest Service sales. This increase in price (both in absolute and percentage terms) reflects the increased differences in the types of timber being sold by the two agencies. The Washington DNR still sells an average-to-good log mix, and Forest Service sales, since the mid 1990s, have been mostly thinning sales containing smaller and lower quality timber. This conclusion is similar to one drawn by Spelter (2005) who observed that lower quality timber and more environmentally constrained logging are two likely reasons for generally lower Forest Service stumpage values.

Discussion

Different messages emerge from this review of timber markets. One of the most powerful is that the stumpage market works with little oversight to allocate resources among buyers and sellers. Its volatility is a testament to its competitive nature—a hallmark feature embraced by economists. There is a concern that with the diminished levels of public sales, a smaller proportion of timber is sold using open process. There is no evidence yet to weigh the consequences of this on the market's competitive nature.

Market forces are working with little fanfare to change the character of forest resources in the PNW. Some of these market forces are highly evident like overall economic performance, and some forces, although highly visible like public timber flows, have a variety of visible and invisible consequences. Still other changes taking place outside the region are having large consequences in the PNW. In the 1980s, the specter of rapid increases in southern lumber production and softwood lumber imports changed the competitive position of the PNW. Currently,

The stumpage market's volatility is a testament to its competitive nature.

international market forces are once again causing the U.S. forest sector to change (see Haynes et al. 2007, Ince et al. 2007 for more discussion of these changes).

Implications of Competitive Markets

One consequence of the competitive nature of stumpage markets is the ability to assume that there is market arbitrage across broad spatial extents, species, quality, and different (but related) products. Market arbitrage is a powerful force that keeps prices of different species, grades, and locations within some fixed proportion to each other. Abstracting from transportation and transactions costs, for example, we conclude that prices of one species and grade will not exceed prices for other species of a similar grade in the long run because of possibilities of substitution.

Market arbitrage has been illustrated working three different ways; across space, species, and quality. A fourth way of using market arbitrage is to describe the price implications for a set of products that have incomplete price reporting. One example of this is the use of export chip prices as a proxy for nonsawtimber prices in the PNW. Prices for nonsawtimber markets are increasingly relevant for forest management that involves nonsawtimber material such as small-diameter trees (those with average diameter at breast height of about 8 inches, in contrast to commercial saw logs that are 4.5 to 11 inches small-end diameter). Available prices for this small-diameter material are limited both in space and time. The only series (for chips) that has been reported consistently for decades are export chip series. Both Haynes (1999) and Busby (2006) found that there was sufficient arbitrage between the export chip and domestic chip markets so that price trends from the export market could be used to describe both markets. That is, inferences about price trends for nonsawtimber material can be developed by observing the trends for export chips (the actual data are published in table 50 of Warren 2006) and adjusting them to local conditions.[11]

Finally, because it is a competitive market, we can see how markets have reacted to interventions such as a small business sales program that restricted competition. In this case, the market responses reveal the costs of good intentions. Market changes can also be used to judge who wins and loses from various changes in market determinants. One example, is the case of restrictions that kept federal logs from export markets. Private landowners who were able to sell logs for export received higher prices than they would have if there had not been restrictions. In this case, they were winners in that they saw increased returns to forestry, and the public (who were the losers) saw reduced returns to forestry.

---

[11] This adjustment is often in the form of a "bridge" relationship that describes local prices as a function of export prices for the closest customs district.

Long-Term Price Trends

Over the past century, persistently rising stumpage prices (table 2) have provided adequate returns to maintain or expand forests and forest management. This improved forest management and protection has created a vast forested commons that produces a wide range of ecosystem goods and services, many of which are free to those who choose to enjoy them. But the recent weakening of expected returns for forest management raises concerns about whether North American forests can meet societal expectations both for making progress toward sustainable forest management (see Haynes 2004, 2007) and for the provision of ecosystem services expected by increasingly urbanized populations. Economists agree that markets can allocate ecosystem services (such as those provided by open space) and monetize values so that they accrue to the landowner.

Advocates for implementing sustainable forest management (SFM) in the United States are lamenting that these weaker prices will reduce market incentives. They are concerned that landowners who are sensitive to investment returns will invest less or convert forest land to higher and better uses. This will increase the dependence on regulatory actions to insure necessary forest practice believed to make progress toward SFM. At the same time, conservation proponents are advocating forest management regimes (e.g., longer rotations) that lead to reduced financial returns and will reduce the adoptions of these management regimes by those landowners who are sensitive to investment returns.

Reduced expectations for the long-term rate of stumpage price appreciation also work against proponents of forest management regimes that embody longer rotations. Such regimes are being advocated by those who see longer rotations as promoting greater biodiversity or greater carbon sequestration. But reduced price expectations lead to lower financial returns and shorter rotations.

Investors are attracted to forestry because of the possibility for high returns (see table in app. 3), but others have noted timber is a relatively risky investment that should be no more than 10 percent of a diverse investment portfolio (Hancock Timber Resource Group 2003). Figure 14 illustrates this riskiness;[12] less risky investments would be in the lower left corner. But in an economic sense, riskiness usually offers the possibility of higher returns, and forest investments have resulted in such higher returns to some investors. For example, figure 14 illustrates the possibility of higher returns from ponderosa pine than other types of timber.

Markets cannot be planned into existence.

---

[12] Riskiness is defined here using an approach that mimics the John Hancock Timber Index (Hancock Timber Resource Group 2003), which is a reconstructed timber returns series.

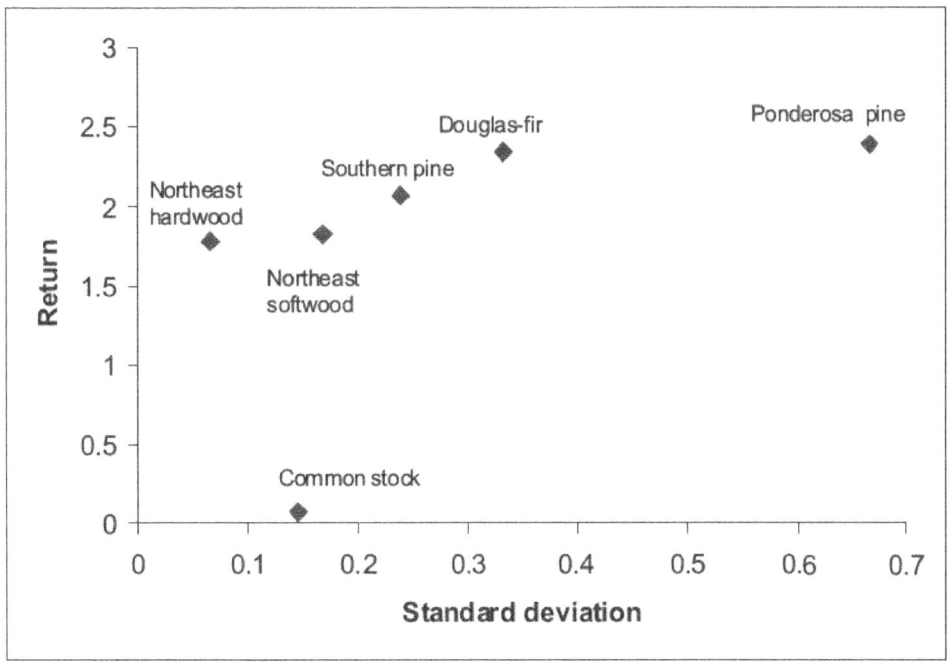

Figure 14—Risk and return of owning U.S. timberland with different timber types, 1963-2002. (Common stock: Thompson 1997).

Market Frustrations

In much of contemporary forest management, planners have frequently misunderstood the nature of markets. Markets cannot be planned into existence nor their evolution taken for granted. Neither is the case. Markets are relatively organic and spring into existence where there is a need for exchange. This organic nature of market emergence has led to two misperceptions that are evident in some contemporary forest management issues.

In the case of nontimber forest products, for example, there is a concern that there are no markets for some of these products (McLain et al., in press). This leads to a number of issues including how to value permits; price reporting; establishing grades; the structure of buyers, sellers, and processors/distributors; and the unregulated nature of the market, making it difficult for sellers, processors, and distributors to compete for capital. This lack of structure complicates management of nontimber forest products including attempts to introduce sustainable practices.

In some of the discussions of ecosystem services, there are occasional references to market failures when discussing the apparent lack of values for such services as clean air or open space. But these are not market failures in the economic sense where the lack of information leads to the failure of markets for efficient allocation; instead, references like this reflect judgments about when market valuation does not produce prices that reflect the value of essential services. The case of clean air (or water) is about the value of a public good. These are societal values and not values established by transactions.

Finally, our forests today exhibit the evidence of how market forces have influenced their extent, composition, structure, and ownership. In forest management, these forces play out sometimes over several decades. Often forest management advocates extol the role progressive forest management has played in reshaping today's forests. While not to diminish that role of progressive forest management, it is the "pull" of markets that have enabled the utilization of material available from forest management and led to increased returns to forest management.

Implications for Ecosystem Service Markets

What implications or lessons do timber markets offer for the emerging arena of ecosystem services? Foremost is the role of property rights. For a buyer or seller to be able to enjoy the benefits of exchange, they must have the right to sell a unique good or service. Whether it is a thousand board feet of timber or a single animal unit month of forage, the seller has the property right. That is, they own it and are free to exchange it.

Nearly as important is the issue of measurable units. Can we describe the units of various goods and services? For consumable goods these are fairly descriptive units such as a thousand board feet of timber, pounds of mushrooms, bunches of salal, animal unit months of forage, but for nonconsumerable goods these are less distinct such as recreation visitor days, clean water in streams, landscape attractiveness, improved habitat, etc.

Related to this is the valuation question. To value something in an economic sense, you need to measure the value. This paper has focused on timber values and how they are set in the market place and are affected by different types of market interventions and issues. Timber is measured as price per thousand board feet or other units (cords, or tons). Without being able to measure a service, you have to rely on social values—still important but not set in markets. That is not to say that valuation of these nonmarket goods is impossible, just that it is subject to less precise methods.

Another implication is the role of transaction data and the richness they add to the discussion of markets. Transaction data give us detail about market prices and quantities as well as details about the buyers and sellers.

Conclusion

This review has shown that markets are powerful institutions that can sweep aside the best-laid plans. Timber markets are highly competitive, volatile, and change relentlessly. They adjust across space and time as suppliers and consumers enter and leave the market as technical changes alter costs.

The long-term price trends support the notion that increasing scarcity of sawtimber and high-quality material will result in higher prices. In general, the relative prices among species and regions have remained unchanged. Price arbitrage and substitution between products, however, act to limit the extent that prices for selected species and different locations can increase. The fact that prices generally increase more for higher priced items than for lower priced items is significant to forest land management decisions, because it is the dollar difference, not the percentage difference, that determines how much can be spent in forest management to increase quality to gain a price premium.

The organic nature of markets will continue to frustrate those who expect structure and order. But for those who do understand the transitory nature of markets, there are opportunities to use these powerful forces to change forest resources. The evidence of that power is all around us in the third forest that is emerging in the PNW.

The power of markets is demonstrated in the third forest that is emerging around us.

Metric Equivalents

When you know:	Multiply by:	To get:
Cubic feet	0.2	Board feet
Cubic feet	.028	Cubic meters
Inches	2.54	Cenitmeters
Miles	1.609	Kilometers

Species List

Common name	Scientific name
Cedar	*Chamaecyparis* Spach
Douglas-fir	*Pseudotsuga menziesii* (Mirbel.) Franco
Engelmann spruce	*Picea engelmanni* Parry ex Engelm.
Larch	*Larix* P. Mill.
Lodgepole pine	*Pinus contorta* Dougl. ex Loud
Ponderosa pine	*Pinus ponderosa* P. & C. Lawson
True fir	*Abies* P. Mill.
Western hemlock	*Tsuga heterophylla* (Raf.) Sarg.
Western white pine	*Pinus monticola* Dougl. ex D. Don

References

Adams, D.M.; Haynes, R.W. 1989. A model of national forest timber supply and stumpage markets in the Western United States. Forest Science. 85(2): 410–424.

Adams, D.M.; Haynes, R.W. 1996. The 1993 timber assessment market model: structure, projections and policy simulations. Gen. Tech. Rep. PNW-GTR-368. Portland, OR: U.S. Department of Agriculture, Forest Service, Pacific Northwest Research Station. 58 p.

Adams, D.M.; Haynes, R.W.; Daigneault, A.J. 2006. Estimated timber harvest by U.S. region and ownership, 1950-2002. Gen. Tech. Rep. PNW-GTR-659. Portland, OR: U.S. Department of Agriculture, Forest Service, Pacific Northwest Research Station. 64 p.

Barbour, R.J.; Haynes, R.W.; Martin, J.R.; Lee, D.C.; White, R.; Bormann, B.T. 2006. Context for the Northwest Forest Plan. In: Haynes, R.W.; Bormann, B.T.; Lee, D.C.; Martin, J.R., tech. eds. 2006. Northwest Forest Plan—the first 10 years (1994-2003): synthesis of monitoring and research results. Gen. Tech. Rep. PNW-GTR-651. Portland, OR: U.S. Department of Agriculture, Forest Service, Pacific Northwest Research Station: 11–22. Chapter 2.

Barbour, R.J.; Marshall, D.D.; Lowell, E.C. 2003. Managing for wood quality. In: Monserud, R.A.; Haynes, R.W.; Johnson, A.C., eds. Compatible forest management. Dordrecht, The Netherlands: Kluwer Academic Publishers: 299–336. Chapter 11.

Bressler, R.G., Jr.; King, R.A. 1970. Markets, prices and interregional trade. New York: John Wiley and Sons, Inc. 426 p.

Busby, G.M. 2006. Export chip prices as a proxy for nonsawtimber prices in the Pacific Northwest. Res. Note. PNW-RN-554. Portland, OR: U.S. Department of Agriculture, Forest Service, Pacific Northwest Research Station. 14 p.

Daniels, J.M. 2005. The rise and fall of the Pacific Northwest export market. Gen. Tech. Rep. PNW-GTR-624. Portland, OR: U.S. Department of Agriculture, Forest Service, Pacific Northwest Research Station. 80 p.

Darr, D.R.; Haynes, R.W.; Adams, D.M. 1980. The impact of the export and import of raw logs on domestic timber supplies and prices. Res. Pap. PNW-277. Portland, OR: U.S. Department of Agriculture, Forest Service, Pacific Northwest Research Station. 38 p.

Fackler, P.F.; Goodwin, B.K. 2001. Spatial price analysis. In: Gardner, B.; Rauser, G., eds. Handbook of agricultural economics. Amsterdam, The Netherlands: Elsevier ScienceBV: 971-1024. Chapter 17. Vol. 1.

Fisher, D.M. 1996. The great wave price: revolutions and the rhythm of history. New York: Oxford University Press. 536 p.

George, P.S.; King, G.A. 1971. Consumer demand for food commodities in the United States with projections for 1980. Giannini Foundation Monograph 26. Berkeley, CA: California Agriculture Experiment Station. 161 p.

Hancock Timber Resource Group. 2003. Historical returns for timberland: research notes 2003. N-03-3. Boston, MA: Hancock Timber Resource Group. 11 p.

Haynes, R.W. 1977. A derived demand approach to estimating the linkage between stumpage and lumber markets. Forest Science. 23(2): 281–288.

Haynes, R.W. 1979. A comparison of open and set-aside timber sales on National Forests in the Douglas-fir region. Land Economics. 55: 277–284.

Haynes, R.W. 1980. Competition for national forest timber in the Northern, Pacific Southwest and Pacific Northwest regions. Res. Pap. PNW-RP-266. Portland, OR: U.S. Department of Agriculture, Forest Service, Pacific Northwest Research Station. 72 p.

Haynes, R.W. 1986. Inventory and value of old-growth in the Douglas-fir region. Res. Note PNW-437. Portland, OR: U.S. Department of Agriculture, Forest Service, Pacific Northwest Research Station. 18 p.

Haynes, R.W. 1991. Monthly stumpage prices for the Pacific Northwest. Res. Pap. PNW-RP-436. Portland, OR: U.S. Department of Agriculture, Forest Service, Pacific Northwest Research Station. 14 p.

Haynes, R.W. 1999. Export chip prices as a proxy for non-sawtimber prices in the Pacific Northwest. Res. Note. PNW-RN-537. Portland, OR: U.S. Department of Agriculture, Forest Service, Pacific Northwest Research Station. 25 p.

Haynes, R.W., tech. ed. 2003. An analysis of the timber situation in the United States: 1952 to 2050. A technical document supporting the 2000 USDA Forest Service RPA Assessment. Gen. Tech. Rep. PNW-GTR-560. Portland, OR: U.S. Department of Agriculture, Forest Service, Pacific Northwest Research Station. 254 p.

Haynes, R.W. 2004. Do markets provide barriers or incentives for sustainable forest management? The US experience. In: One forest under two flags. SAF convention proceedings. [CD ROM]. Bethesda, MD: Society of American Foresters.

Haynes, R.W. 2005. Economic feasibility of longer management regimes in the Douglas-fir region. Res. Note PNW-RN-547. Portland, OR: U.S. Department of Agriculture, Forest Service, Pacific Northwest Research Station. 14 p.

Haynes, R.W. 2007. Integrating concerns about wood production and sustainable forest management in the United States. In: Deal, R.L.; White, R.; Benson, G., eds. Emerging issues for sustainable forest management. Journal of Sustainable Forestry. 24(1): 1–18.

Haynes, R.W.; Adams, D.M. 2007. Evolving views of the future of the U.S. forest sector. In: Adams, D.M.; Haynes, R.W., eds. The utility of forest sector models in addressing forest policy questions. Dordrecht, The Netherlands: Springer: 353–380. Chapter 10.

Haynes, R.W.; Adams, D.M.; Alig, R.J.; Ince, P.J.; Mills, J.R.; Zhou, X. 2007. The 2005 RPA timber assessment update. Gen. Tech. Rep. PNW-GTR-699. Portland, OR: U.S. Department of Agriculture, Forest Service, Pacific Northwest Research Station. 212 p.

Haynes, R.W.; Fahey, T.D.; Fight, R.D. 1988. Price projections for selected grades of Douglas-fir lumber. Res. Note. PNW-RN-473. Portland, OR: U.S. Department of Agriculture, Forest Service, Pacific Northwest Research Station. 10 p.

Haynes, R.W.; Fight, R.D. 2004. Reconsidering price projections for selected grades of Douglas-fir, coast hem-fir, inland hem-fir, and ponderosa pine lumber. Res. Pap. PNW-RP-561. Portland, OR: U.S. Department of Agriculture, Forest Service, Pacific Northwest Research Station. 31 p.

Howard, J.L. 2003. U.S. timber production, trade, consumption, and price statistics 1965-2002. Res. Pap. FPL-RP-615. Madison, WI: U.S. Department of Agriculture, Forest Service, Forest Products Laboratory. 90 p.

Ince, P.J.; Schuler, A.; Spelter, H.; Luppold, W. 2007. Globalization and structural change in the U.S. forest sector: an evolving context for sustainable forest management. Gen. Tech. Rep. FPL-GTR-170. Madison, WI: U.S. Department of Agriculture, Forest Service, Forest Products Laboratory. 62 p.

Log Lines. [2000-2004]. Log price reporting service. Mount Vernon, WA. Monthly.

Mason, D.T. 1969. Memoirs of a forester, part III. Forest History. 13(1&2): 28–39.

McLain, R.J.; Alexander, S.J.; Jones, E.T. [In press]. Incorporating understanding of informal economic activity in natural resource and economic development policy. Gen. Tech. Rep. PNW-GTR-755. Portland, OR: U.S. Department of Agriculture, Forest Service, Pacific Northwest Research Station.

Mead, W.J. 1966. Competition and oligopsony in the Douglas-fir lumber industry. Berkeley, CA: University of California Press. 276 p.

Random Lengths Yardstick. 2007. The monthly measure of forest product statistics. Random Lengths Publications, Inc.: 17(4): 1.

Sendak, P.E. 1994. Northeast regional timber stumpage prices: 1961-91. Res. Pap. NE-683. Radnor, PA: U.S. Department of Agriculture, Forest Service, Northeastern Forest Experiment Station. 6 p.

Sohngen, B.L.; Haynes, R.W. 1994. The "great" price spike of '93: an analysis of lumber and stumpage prices in the Pacific Northwest. Res. Pap. PNW-RP-471. Portland, OR: U.S. Department of Agriculture, Forest Service, Pacific Northwest Research Station. 20 p.

Spelter, H. 2005. Review of alternative measures of softwood sawtimber prices in the United States. Res. Pap. FPL-RP-629. Madison, WI: U.S. Department of Agriculture, Forest Service, Forest Products Laboratory. 16 p.

Spies, T.A. 2006. Maintaining old-growth forests. In: Haynes, R.W.; Bormann, B.T.; Lee, D.C.; Martin, J.R., tech. eds. Northwest Forest Plan—the first 10 years (1994-2003): synthesis of monitoring and research results. Gen. Tech. Rep. PNW-GTR-651. Portland, OR: U.S. Department of Agriculture, Forest Service, Pacific Northwest Research Station: 83–115. Chapter 6.

Thomson, T.A. 1997. Long-term portfolio returns from timber and financial assets. Journal of Real Estate Portfolio Management. 3(1): 57–73.

Timber Mart-South. [2000-2004]. The journal of southern timber prices. Athens, GA: Timber Mart-South; Center for Forest Business, Daniel B. Warnell School of Forestry and Natural Resources, University of Georgia. [Irregular pagination]. Quarterly.

U.S. Department of Agriculture, Forest Service [USDA FS]. 1973. The outlook for timber in the United States. Forest Resour. Rep. 20. Washington, DC: U.S. Government Printing Office. 224 p. [plus appendixies].

U.S. Department of Agriculture, Forest Service; U.S. Department of the Interior, Bureau of Land Management [USDA and USDI]. 1994. Record of decision for amendments to Forest Service and Bureau of Land Management planning documents within the range of the northern spotted owl. [Place of publication unknown]. 74 p. [plus attachment A: standards and guidelines].

Waggener, T.R.; Fight, R.D. 1999. Clearwood quality and softwood lumber prices: what is the real premium? Western Journal of Applied Forestry. 14(2): 73–79.

Warren, D.D. 2004. Production, prices, employment and trade in Northwest forest industries, all quarters 2002. Resour. Bull. PNW-RB-241. Portland, OR: U.S. Department of Agriculture, Forest Service, Pacific Northwest Research Station. 171 p.

Warren, D.D. 2006. Production, prices, employment and trade in Northwest forest industries, all quarters 2004. Resour. Bull. PNW-RB-250. Portland, OR: U.S. Department of Agriculture, Forest Service, Pacific Northwest Research Station. 165 p.

Weigand, J.F.; Haynes, R.W.; Mikowski, J.L., eds. 1994. High quality forestry workshop: the idea of long rotations. Proceedings. CINTRAFOR SP-15. Seattle, WA: College of Forest Resources, University of Washington. 267 p.

Appendix 1: Long-Term Data Sets

Table 3—Softwood stumpage and lumber prices for Douglas-fir, ponderosa pine, and southern pine

Year	Douglas-fir		Ponderosa pine		Southern pine	
	Stumpage	Lumber	Stumpage	Lumber	Stumpage	Lumber
	1982 dollars/thousand board feet					
1910	33.79	107.72	24.40	117.28	13.04	109.37
1911	34.75	98.89	18.41	121.89	25.64	124.10
1912	34.09	95.06	18.26	111.80	13.04	117.87
1913	32.27	71.53	15.06	96.47	14.81	80.66
1914	32.08	68.98	14.01	89.43	25.28	141.38
1915	36.15	88.53	17.22	119.70	18.22	103.74
1916	29.98	73.17	16.20	98.56	22.34	97.28
1917	29.88	80.42	8.95	96.77	17.48	93.86
1918	29.91	83.17	9.85	92.46	14.00	108.02
1919	30.72	103.17	10.36	116.29	16.20	120.33
1920	29.44	130.03	11.47	145.60	17.19	134.91
1921	31.19	107.31	15.69	160.33	22.62	115.54
1922	32.61	125.69	19.79	166.65	17.48	142.07
1923	32.38	155.60	18.50	190.78	17.97	171.92
1924	31.85	130.87	17.07	164.34	21.38	157.34
1925	31.06	117.52	16.65	155.48	18.61	148.50
1926	31.74	116.92	17.66	154.37	21.48	153.83
1927	32.68	118.14	17.01	158.17	21.87	144.37
1928	33.51	114.01	12.34	157.93	22.19	147.46
1929	33.16	122.25	18.08	161.41	21.95	156.47
1930	35.35	113.56	19.91	157.96	22.12	141.44
1931	35.71	95.93	27.54	163.05	27.62	135.27
1932	32.66	94.85	19.10	150.63	25.57	118.86
1933	30.90	119.40	20.30	163.41	24.36	157.60
1934	31.31	125.06	15.96	158.92	23.08	167.66
1935	31.58	115.84	14.34	147.96	33.16	132.28
1936	32.65	127.01	13.02	156.89	37.13	149.19
1937	30.98	132.40	12.19	165.09	36.14	149.28
1938	33.93	127.72	15.21	164.16	54.23	140.45
1939	33.20	134.82	14.88	171.26	44.05	148.29
1940	33.37	143.98	13.38	179.43	33.73	157.72
1941	36.02	169.13	14.22	190.39	71.87	169.46
1942	35.49	155.90	15.88	180.47	62.88	166.56
1943	37.06	158.20	28.14	181.31	58.86	167.77
1944	42.08	170.00	22.34	191.90	72.99	178.14
1945	41.23	169.04	30.71	190.19	61.27	176.63
1946	43.46	170.21	27.83	186.95	51.44	174.52
1947	41.70	250.69	26.74	227.37	43.06	269.19
1948	54.42	264.31	43.44	262.37	59.52	272.75

Table 3—Softwood stumpage and lumber prices for Douglas-fir, ponderosa pine, and southern pine (continued)

Year	Douglas-fir		Ponderosa pine		Southern pine	
	Stumpage	Lumber	Stumpage	Lumber	Stumpage	Lumber
	1982 dollars/thousand board feet					
1949	43.04	243.17	55.15	263.92	75.03	259.31
1950	40.37	287.47	55.19	289.36	97.80	279.98
1951	49.57	281.62	90.90	304.13	113.82	269.28
1952	55.03	285.47	76.26	308.56	130.07	279.76
1953	49.11	265.78	73.08	315.84	117.12	281.17
1954	46.96	267.53	76.59	298.50	101.37	268.08
1955	55.15	292.08	73.26	309.28	109.22	277.99
1956	78.32	281.27	73.95	320.84	123.43	278.71
1957	70.29	243.75	63.95	284.58	100.96	260.42
1958	64.05	233.59	49.76	270.24	98.42	252.93
1959	63.69	264.25	53.56	293.44	111.04	260.90
1960	71.42	244.66	49.61	277.81	108.83	256.50
1961	68.70	233.54	31.52	256.17	84.81	246.21
1962	63.06	238.81	41.81	261.25	82.02	245.22
1963	62.50	244.81	41.15	266.21	79.43	245.16
1964	63.61	247.89	49.51	268.67	87.97	245.44
1965	70.22	241.35	61.30	262.91	98.14	244.46
1966	86.34	246.64	59.46	264.25	115.92	260.50
1967	115.93	248.00	66.47	260.60	114.67	259.28
1968	106.96	288.44	88.30	297.58	123.39	287.78
1969	125.70	306.92	199.44	361.92	145.22	306.01
1970	104.31	243.74	86.99	294.97	119.51	268.70
1971	108.43	290.47	98.69	336.77	137.01	304.12
1972	122.96	324.72	165.33	381.93	164.82	329.62
1973	114.44	384.71	205.11	439.82	207.56	298.96
1974	122.34	305.03	188.04	348.40	142.43	198.26
1975	121.64	257.67	121.92	293.91	97.60	155.89
1976	155.50	306.87	166.61	351.24	142.39	182.54
1977	179.35	369.15	202.47	356.13	144.84	326.13
1978	191.57	379.41	235.62	375.24	170.24	345.24
1979	181.02	402.33	303.68	356.27	186.79	321.27
1980	158.62	324.54	229.51	262.27	138.08	218.96
1981	138.05	259.23	199.18	196.93	138.78	151.93
1982	87.06	215.14	66.90	162.85	124.00	127.85
1983	94.80	232.21	102.67	231.45	141.16	186.45
1984	96.93	214.28	118.32	245.08	136.93	200.08
1985	84.57	214.06	98.26	259.69	116.28	214.69
1986	98.95	218.03	156.29	273.67	118.76	228.67
1987	115.35	231.36	203.60	294.58	105.32	249.58
1988	155.58	241.30	170.35	307.55	116.46	262.55
1989	172.62	257.29	260.25	285.07	106.73	240.07
1990	204.58	235.57	217.79	310.01	110.28	265.01

Table 3—Softwood stumpage and lumber prices for Douglas-fir, ponderosa pine, and southern pine (continued)

Year	Douglas-fir		Ponderosa pine		Southern pine	
	Stumpage	Lumber	Stumpage	Lumber	Stumpage	Lumber
			1982 dollars/thousand board feet			
1991	224.16	230.70	203.95	267.59	109.01	207.59
1992	249.39	265.32	248.98	356.57	136.31	311.57
1993	416.71	390.02	478.28	381.53	158.96	336.53
1994	395.89	346.22	241.43	411.56	205.98	366.56
1995	363.15	302.25	119.44	307.62	214.92	262.62
1996	313.20	339.46	212.26	382.61	185.59	337.61
1997	327.11	341.22	211.59	404.83	228.06	359.83
1998	260.75	280.99	164.18	434.89	244.37	389.89
1999	281.39	322.19	143.08	597.82	231.08	552.82
2000	232.53	266.26	114.69	372.99	221.22	327.99
2001	183.78	247.55	85.11	386.73	195.04	341.73
2002	207.95	246.06	86.49	371.27	209.00	311.27
2003	138.89	242.25	79.94		117.61	
2004	115.18	292.30	44.31		123.98	

The original data for 1910-1972 are a mix of national forest timber sale data and prices for privately owned timber (see table 2, Appendix V USDA FS 1973). Similar data for 1973 to 2004 are found in table 20 of Howard (2003). The data shown here are adjusted from the original data to represent harvest prices for all species (and all owners) in the Douglas-fir region (western Washington and Oregon) and to represent stumpage prices (for all owners) in the South-Central region. The data are deflated using the producer price index (1982 = 100).

Table 4—Prices for Northeastern softwood and hardwood sawtimber

Year	Hardwood	Softwood
	1982 dollars/thousand board feet	
1961	43.171	43.867
1962	43.508	44.811
1963	45.364	47.149
1964	44.874	45.709
1965	45.319	47.907
1966	47.429	47.661
1967	44.641	48.814
1968	47.213	49.056
1969	50.331	51.098
1970	51.894	47.930
1971	49.682	48.979
1972	51.852	48.829
1973	46.709	46.433
1974	74.729	45.527
1975	66.176	48.836
1976	69.532	51.466
1977	74.094	51.057
1978	88.974	54.827
1979	103.793	59.635
1980	88.864	54.705
1981	82.908	49.994
1982	85.669	52.545
1983	103.519	50.528
1984	100.934	50.834
1985	101.600	51.968
1986	113.703	53.241
1987	129.032	56.876
1988	152.801	57.244
1989	127.252	58.381
1990	122.738	57.459
1991	119.942	55.915
1992	145.430	55.944
1993	189.968	60.108
1994	202.689	65.866
1995	185.735	69.276
1996	174.359	69.069
1997	201.666	75.886
1998	207.133	80.276
1999	207.095	85.551
2000	224.379	83.733
2001	199.470	77.944
2002	211.134	78.387

The data for 1961-1991 are from Sendak (1994). He also provided updates for the same series through 2002.

Appendix 2: Price Setting in an Economic Context

Figure 15 illustrates two cases of how economists view price setting. In the most common form (on the right side of fig. 15) the intersection of supply and demand functions (labeled d_x and s_x) are assumed to set the price and quantity (labeled P_1 and Q_1). Such prices and quantities are sometimes called the equilibrium price and quantities because they represent the intersection of the supply and demand functions.

The responsiveness of supply and demand functions in terms of changes in prices is measured by their elasticities (ε). These are computed at some point (P_1, Q_1) as the product of that point and the slope of the supply or demand function.

This relationship is expressed as: $\varepsilon = \dfrac{\Delta Q}{\Delta P} \times \dfrac{P_1}{Q_1}$

Supply elasticities have a positive value reflecting how supply functions slope upward to the right (see fig. 15). Demand elasticities are negative reflecting the downward sloping demand functions. Elasticities are typically described as being inelastic ($\varepsilon < 1.0$) elastic ($\varepsilon > 1.0$), and in rare cases unity ($\varepsilon = 1.0$). There are no units associated with ε. Finally, most studies of stumpage markets have found

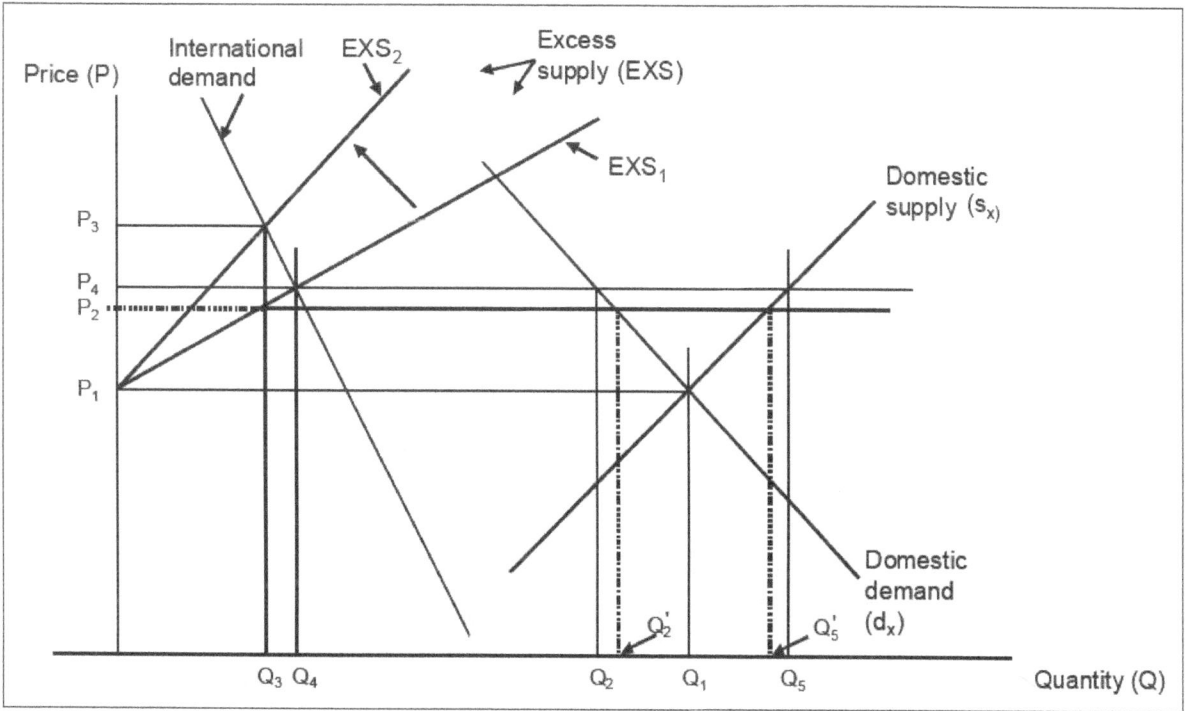

Figure 15—Supply and demand representations showing the price premium for exportable logs.

stumpage to be inelastic (see Adams and Haynes 1996). The implication is that small changes in quantities lead to larger price changes.

Figure 15 can also be used to illustrate how the opportunity for trade affects price setting in single markets (as illustrated in the case of log exports). First, assume that the supply and demand functions (s_x, d_x) represent the U.S. domestic stumpage market. Along the left (the price) axis we have introduced two additional functions. The excess supply function (EXS) is the horizontal distance between the domestic supply and demand functions (i.e., Q_5 - Q_2). Its origin on the price axis is the equilibrium price in the domestic market without trade (P_1). This excess supply function represents the excess U.S. stumpage available at prices above the equilibrium price (P_1). The other new function is the excess demand for stumpage from another market (labeled international demand). In the case of the log export trade, this function would represent the demand in several Pacific Rim markets that import logs from the United States. In the case of two markets or any multiple of markets, equilibrium conditions are set by the intersection of the excess supply and excess demand functions. In this case, the price allowing for trade would be P_4 with quantity Q_4 being exported and the quantity Q_2 being consumed in the domestic market. Total production for both markets is Q_5. Important to note is that in the presence of trade, prices rise in the domestic market (from P_1 to P_4), consumption falls (from Q_1 to Q_2), and total production, increases from Q_1 to Q_5. Not illustrated here, prices fall in the importing regions and consumption expands with the advent of trade among the regions.

Figure 15 also illustrates the market effects of restrictions on the export of federal logs. These restrictions shift the excess supply curve (EXS) back toward the price axis (from EXS_1 to EXS_2). The amount of this shift is the volume restricted from export. The bifurcation of the market results in a higher price (P_3) for logs that can be exported and a lower price (P_2) for stumpage restricted to the domestic market. In both cases, prices are higher than without trade where the price would be P_1. The difference $P_3 - P_2$ is the export price premium.

With log export restrictions, there are reductions in both the volume of log exports from Q_4 to Q_3 and in total production. But with lower prices, domestic consumption increases from Q_2 to Q_2'. Even those landowners whose logs are restricted from export benefit as prices rise from P_1 to P_2. This increase in prices partially explains the higher prices for federal sales in the Pacific Northwest relative to other regions.

Appendix 3: Rate of Return Data Set

Table 5—Rates of return for Douglas-fir, southern pine, ponderosa pine, northeast softwood, and northeast hardwood stumpage

Year	Douglas-fir	Southern pine	Ponderosa pine	Northeast hardwood	Northeast softwood
		Percent per year			
1912	2.24	1.61	2.02		
1913	2.16	1.65	1.98		
1914	2.20	3.06	2.00		
1915	2.44	1.89	2.53		
1916	2.07	2.04	2.30		
1917	2.10	1.82	1.55		
1918	2.25	1.59	1.89		
1919	2.29	2.04	2.40		
1920	2.21	2.18	2.45		
1921	2.31	2.47	2.90		
1922	2.36	1.84	2.90		
1923	2.27	1.86	2.31		
1924	2.22	2.27	2.09		
1925	2.20	1.93	2.15		
1926	2.26	2.10	2.32		
1927	2.31	2.12	2.24		
1928	2.31	2.03	1.82		
1929	2.25	1.99	2.62		
1930	2.34	2.00	2.69		
1931	2.31	2.34	2.91		
1932	2.13	2.04	1.97		
1933	2.10	1.89	2.04		
1934	2.23	1.90	1.97		
1935	2.27	2.54	1.92		
1936	2.31	2.40	2.04		
1937	2.20	2.04	2.08		
1938	2.35	2.64	2.56		
1939	2.28	1.97	2.37		
1940	2.24	1.57	2.08		
1941	2.37	3.18	2.26		
1942	2.28	2.23	2.47		
1943	2.30	1.83	3.53		
1944	2.49	2.27	2.27		
1945	2.31	1.91	2.59		
1946	2.32	1.68	2.32		
1947	2.23	1.68	2.12		
1948	2.67	2.36	3.14		
1949	2.10	2.59	3.04		

Table 5—Rates of return for Douglas-fir, southern pine, ponderosa pine, northeast softwood, and northeast hardwood stumpage (continued)

Year	Douglas-fir	Southern pine	Ponderosa pine	Northeast hardwood	Northeast softwood
			Percent per year		
1950	1.98	2.58	2.42		
1951	2.54	2.41	3.22		
1952	2.57	2.30	2.31		
1953	2.16	1.95	2.06		
1954	2.10	1.76	2.29		
1955	2.47	2.00	2.22		
1956	3.03	2.23	2.23		
1957	2.33	1.83	2.05		
1958	2.04	1.83	1.82		
1959	2.17	2.15	2.16		
1960	2.43	2.05	2.19		
1961	2.27	1.69	1.66		
1962	2.10	1.79	2.30		
1963	2.17	1.94	2.43	1.80	1.82
1964	2.27	2.12	2.54	1.76	1.74
1965	2.42	2.23	2.76	1.76	1.79
1966	2.68	2.32	2.36	1.81	1.77
1967	2.95	2.09	2.40	1.71	1.78
1968	2.33	2.09	2.84	1.78	1.77
1969	2.44	2.29	4.51	1.86	1.80
1970	2.10	1.86	1.72	1.82	1.70
1971	2.16	2.05	1.71	1.72	1.74
1972	2.48	2.37	3.40	1.77	1.76
1973	2.23	2.49	3.02	1.66	1.69
1974	2.30	1.70	2.27	2.36	1.70
1975	2.29	1.37	1.67	1.85	1.82
1976	2.66	2.27	2.37	1.73	1.85
1977	2.67	2.26	2.83	1.86	1.77
1978	2.46	2.25	2.65	2.03	1.83
1979	2.21	2.24	2.82	2.06	1.90
1980	2.03	1.70	2.04	1.66	1.70
1981	1.96	1.80	1.85	1.58	1.60
1982	1.62	1.86	1.19	1.75	1.75
1983	1.99	2.10	1.84	2.01	1.73
1984	2.35	2.04	2.80	1.83	1.73
1985	2.07	1.78	2.09	1.74	1.78
1986	2.39	1.92	2.94	1.89	1.79
1987	2.63	1.86	3.09	1.98	1.84
1988	2.91	2.05	2.17	2.05	1.80
1989	2.64	1.95	2.86	1.64	1.78
1990	2.61	1.98	2.27	1.60	1.74
1991	2.53	2.01	2.02	1.70	1.71
1992	2.49	2.32	2.52	1.98	1.73

Table 5—Rates of return for Douglas-fir, southern pine, ponderosa pine, northeast softwood, and northeast hardwood stumpage (continued)

Year	Douglas-fir	Southern pine	Ponderosa pine	Northeast hardwood	Northeast softwood
			Percent per year		
1993	3.37	2.38	3.86	2.24	1.84
1994	2.51	2.51	1.79	1.98	1.91
1995	2.09	2.23	1.12	1.69	1.86
1996	1.98	1.84	2.55	1.63	1.78
1997	2.20	2.19	2.63	1.89	1.86
1998	1.97	2.23	1.91	1.87	1.87
1999	2.18	1.97	1.88	1.77	1.86
2000	2.04	1.91	1.86	1.85	1.76
2001	1.81	1.82	1.72	1.66	1.66
2002	2.25	2.01	2.04	1.75	1.71
2003	1.82	1.45	2.15		
2004	1.71	1.65	1.54		

These were computed as:

$$\text{rate of return} = \frac{\left(\text{income rate} \times \text{price}_t\right) + \left([2\,\text{price}_t + \text{price}_{t-1}]/3\right)}{\left(2\,\text{price}_{t-1} + \text{price}_{t-2}\right)/3} - 1$$

The income rates are 1.25 for Douglas-fir and ponderosa pine, 1.00 for southern pine and 0.75 for northern species. See Hancock (2003) for details for the various assumptions.